GOVZILLA

How The Relentless Growth Of Government Is Devouring Our Economy - And Our Freedom

STEPHEN MOORE

Post Hill
PRESS

A POST HILL PRESS BOOK
ISBN: 978-1-63758-384-5
ISBN (eBook): 978-1-63758-385-2

Govzilla:
How the Relentless Growth of Government Is Devouring
Our Economy—And Our Freedom
© 2021 by Stephen Moore
All Rights Reserved

Interior Design by Yoni Limor

Post Hill Press
New York • Nashville
posthillpress.com

Published in the United States of America
1 2 3 4 5 6 7 8 9 10

"A government that is big enough to give you everything you want is big enough to take everything you've got."

—Ronald Reagan

Table of Contents

Foreword

BY SENATOR RAND PAUL OF KENTUCKY

September 2, 2021

When Steve Moore asked me to write the foreword for *Govzilla*, I told him as long as the audience is left with no sympathy for big government, debt, and taxes. Steve assured me that not only is the book in defense of limited, constitutional government, but also the book even trashes the whole concept of a progressive income tax. I said... count me in.

When we were a constitutional republic, the worry of our government transforming into Govzilla was not so paramount. But now, with the courts enforcing very few constitutional restraints on big government, the nanny-state is invading every sphere of our personal lives.

Most voters are unaware of Thomas Paine's admonition that "government is a necessary evil." Necessary to avoid the chaos of violence that no government might allow and evil because we must give up some of our liberty to have government.

We give up that liberty in many forms but primarily in the form of taxes. If we allow the government to take 50 percent of our earnings, we are, in essence only 50 percent free. The argument for preserving liberty is easier to make when everyone works, as they have a self-interest in their liberty to keep most of what they earn.

The problem comes when the nonworking class becomes larger and larger and becomes a majority. When constitutional restraints fall away and majority rule takes over, liberty becomes subservient to the whims of those who live off of government largesse. Without the self-interest of preserving the fruits of their earnings, the majority increasingly votes for more "free" stuff.

This situation translates into deficits and debt until the weight of the debt becomes an anchor dragging us all into the malaise of a stagnant economy and interest payments that consume more and more of tax revenue.

The greater the debt becomes, the greater our taxes become, the less free we become.

Which party is to blame? Republicans?…well, yes. Democrats?…well, yes. In fact, there's enough blame to go around. Most Republicans in Congress vote for unlimited military spending and most Democrats in Congress vote for unlimited social welfare spending. The unholy alliance produces compromise and all categories of spending go up each year.

Compounding the problem is that the Demopublican support for spending is then dwarfed by the entitlement spending that is growing even more rapidly than the discretionary budget that Congress votes on each year.

The budget voted on by Congress is about one third of total spending. Two thirds of spending is categorized as entitlement or mandatory spending and is never voted on. Mandatory spending includes things like Medicare, Medicaid, food stamps. These programs are never reformed. In fact, they are never voted on at all.

I came face to face with this problem shortly after I arrived in the Senate. I discovered that Social Security was $7 trillion in debt. I proposed to make Social Security sound for seventy-five years by gradually raising the age of retirement to seventy over twenty years and instituting means testing for how much each individual received, those with higher incomes would receive a greater "hair-cut."

I got only three co-sponsors, all Republicans. The big-government Republicans who perpetually harangued that they would not vote to cut on-budget spending because the real problem was "entitlement" spending proved to be disingenuous (liars is the more accurate but less politically correct word). Not one of these Republicans signed on to help "cut" or event "restrain" entitlement spending.

Steve Moore presents the dilemma we face and the immanency of the problem. We must act now to save our Republic or forever rue the day complacency caused us to sit at home complaining but not acting.

Every day in the Senate I put forward my best effort to rein in big government. But I need help. Not one Democrat even pretends to care about the debt, except when putting forward false arguments on tax cuts creating deficits. (Steve Moore does a great job debunking this shibboleth).

But it's not just that Congress needs more Republicans. I volunteered as a teenage intern in my dad's congressional office. I remember going to committee hearings and asking him why the high-ranking members of each committee on both sides of the aisles voted almost identically for big government? He explained that really the mainstream of both parties shared the belief that government is the solution to most problems.

As an intern, I saw firsthand that Republicans never countered the Democrat's deficit-laden budget with a balanced budget. Since I've been in the Senate, I've faithfully put forward a budget that balances in five years. Why five years? Because that's the rule put forward by the constitutional amendment that every Republican in Congress has voted for. Shouldn't we put forward budgets that actually align with the Balanced Budget Amendment we profess to support?

About eight years ago, a freeze in current spending would have balanced the budget in five years. Then a couple of years later, a 1 percent cut in spending each year for five years would have brought us into balance. But it became harder and harder to balance. Big-government Republicans in league with Democrats kept blowing through spending caps until this year it now takes a 5 percent cut annually for five years to bring about balance.

The good news is my "nickel" plan got more votes this year than ever before—twenty-seven. The bad news is that twenty-three big-government Republicans voted against balancing the budget in five years.

Steve Moore's *Govzilla* zeroes in on the exponential growth of government and the urgency of rising up to defend limited, constitutional government. My hope is that this book will inform you, anger you, and ultimately prompt you to help us take back the republic.

Preface

ON SOURCES AND BUDGET ESTIMATES

Unless otherwise noted, all of the historical budget and tax statistics in this book come from the Historical Tables of the United States Budget, published by the Office of Management and Budget or the Congressional Budget Office (CBO).

Unless otherwise indicated, all of the historical statistics are adjusted for inflation and presented in 2020 real dollars.

The starting point for our projections for future outlays, taxes, debt, and deficits are the Congressional Budget Office long-term fiscal forecast through the year 2051. Those numbers already are daunting because of entitlement spending and the demographic reality of some 75 million baby boomers in retirement collecting government payments via Social Security and Medicare. In other words, even without the Biden debt explosion, America faces a budget train wreck.

We adjust these latest CBO projections based on the assumption that the entire $4.5 trillion Biden spending bill (the infrastructure bill and the welfare bill) is adopted, as well as the Biden tax increases. We include some intermediate assumptions, with half of the Biden plan being adopted.

We assume that the dynamic impact of the tax increases (i.e., the negative economic impact of the higher tax rates) will mean that the federal government will raise only half the projected revenues. Even the Joint Tax Committee has estimated that the Biden administration has vastly overstated the revenue gains from its budget and tax proposals.

We use the Committee for a Responsible Federal Budget (CRFB) forecast for the Biden budget path through 2030. That forecast assumes that the Biden budget is passed as proposed. It is the starting point for our estimate of the fiscal path over the ensuing twenty years. We think the fiscal scenario by 2031 will be somewhat worse than CRFB forecasts, but we use their more conservative estimates.

We then assume that at least half of the extra spending in the Biden budget plan is NOT temporary but, rather, permanent and grows at the historical rate of government spending of about 4 percent to 5 percent per year. We base this assumption on several facts: first, the entitlement expansions in health care, Medicaid, food stamps, child credits, are highly unlikely to be reversed once they are enacted into law. Even the Biden administration has boasted that these programs are "forever," and given Washington's almost complete inability to reverse or cutback on federal income transfer programs, this seems a highly defensible assumption.

To estimate future borrowing costs on the tens of trillions of dollars of additional debt over the next three decades, we use the standard CBO projections of rates on Treasury Bills rising to between 3 percent and 4 percent by 2040 and to 4 percent to 5 percent by 2050.

We assume the official long-term economic growth rate used by CBO and the Office of Management and Budget. These are likely to be overestimates of future growth if the Biden debt, spending, and tax increases are approved, as the transfer of wealth and income away from the private sector to the government sector of the economy will have severe negative impacts on the economy.

This is not a "doomsday" scenario, although the forecasts are extremely troubling. Our debt goes from the forecast of 200 percent of GDP to 300 percent of GDP over the next three decades. Federal spending rises to close to 50 percent of our GDP. These are forecasts of what happens if the Biden spending and debt policies are enacted into law as proposed. A major motivation of this book is to wake up Americans and our elected officials to the catastrophe that awaits us IF Congress enacts this new $4.5 trillion package. We hope and pray that this scenario does not come to pass and that Congress rejects the economically and fiscally destructive path.

Introduction

AMERICA THE BANKRUPT

When I first came to Washington, D.C., and started working on federal budget issues as a pimply-faced kid of twenty-four in the year 1984, the entire federal budget was still less than $1 trillion. In 1985 Ronald Reagan introduced the first $1 trillion budget and we were all aghast and ashamed at the magnitude of the federal spending machine. I remember being asked on a TV show: How many zeroes are there in one trillion. I didn't know. I couldn't count up the zeroes that high. (The answer, of course, is twelve.)

Now some thirty-five years later, we have a president in Joe Biden who wants to authorize $10 trillion of spending in his first year in office. That's a $4 trillion-plus budget PLUS $6 trillion more to transform our economy. This isn't a rescue plan for the economy; it's the fiscal equivalent of a nuclear bomb.

How did our nation, founded on principles of LIMITED government with few and enumerated powers enunciated in the American Constitution, come to this moment we are facing now? How did we get from there to here? The message of this book is that this "progressive" plan will put America in great and long-term financial peril. We are playing a financial game of Jenga, with the politicians continuing to add multitrillion-dollar blocks to a tower that we know will crash down. A government as omnipresent and overbearing as Washington is proposing is not just a threat to our prosperity but also to our basic freedoms and civil liberties.

Again, how did we, as responsible and educated citizens, allow this to happen? And what are the dreary implications for America's financial and economic future if we continue down a path to bankruptcy and/or a financial crash landing? As a member of Congress recently admitted to me: "We are like crack cocaine addicts hooked on spending."

This book isn't all doom and gloom. I'm confident we WILL reverse course before it is too late. To those ends, at the end of the book I provide a 21-Step Recovery Program from Our Addiction to Government. But this recovery plan is never going to happen if citizens are pacifists. The nation needs to rise up and revolt (peacefully) against the political class—of both parties—to steer the Titanic away from the looming financial iceberg.

This collapse of what I call our fiscal constitution did not happen overnight. The dam was first broken during the New Deal era of the 1930s under FDR, gained renewed momentum in the 1960s and Lyndon Johnson's "Great Society War on Poverty," expanded still faster in the 1970s under presidents Nixon, Ford, and Carter (it was Nixon who declared in the early 1970s "We are all Keynesians now"), and accelerated still further under Presidents Obama and Trump and their "stimulus" plans using government spending as a recharging station for the economy—with no regard to the financial implications of what they were doing. Ronald Reagan interrupted the stampede of government, and the economy soared with the supply-side tax reductions, deregulations and a time-out on domestic government spending. And we also saw progress under Democratic president Bill Clinton and the Republican Congress led by then-Speaker of the House Newt Gingrich. Under Clinton, government spending fell from 22 percent to 18 percent of GDP and, lo, the economy and stock market soared.

But the pendulum has swung back in the 21st century. It was George W. Bush who agreed to massive bailouts of failed banks, insurance companies, financial institutions, and auto companies. Obama then took over and suggested $800 billion in stimulus funding that stimulated nothing but more government. Then under Joe Biden, as progressives have taken hold of our Congress and White House, we have a president who has declared that MORE government spending will solve every ill of our country: from poverty to climate change to inequality, homelessness, stagnant wages, and global poverty. Families are now eligible for up to $100,000 in government benefits today without anyone working a single hour. Millions more Americans will become entirely DEPENDENT on government for their sustenance. Some call the $6 trillion Biden wants as the "great reset" of the U.S. economy—away from free enterprise and a lurch toward a welfare state and a command and control economy. But none dare call it "socialism."

This is the "transformation" of the American society that Biden and his administrative minions are conspiring to enact. The philosophy is appealing on the surface:

- Live for the moment.

- The sun will come out tomorrow.

- What have our children and grandchildren done for US, anyway?

THE PANDEMIC OF RUNAWAY SPENDING

The crisis that became the springboard for this progressive utopia was the health pandemic called COVID-19.

Up until the moment the virus hit these shores, the condition of the national financial balance sheet of the country was problematic and even daunting—but not dire. We weren't teetering on the verge of collapse.

And then along came Bernie Sanders, Nancy Pelosi, Bernie Sanders, "the Squad," and an army of "progressive" intellectuals who rode on the coattails of Joe Biden— the "centrist" Democrat—or so we were told. We were snookered.

Now they tell us that the path to "American greatness" is to grow the government beyond our wildest imaginations. They capitalized on the pandemic and the fear it struck in the hearts of the American people to spend trillions of dollars—mostly helping their own voters and the business interests that supported them. This virus mutated into, as Bill Clinton's chief of staff Rahm Emmanuel once put it, "a terrible thing to waste."

The left's vision of an America "transformed," into a socialist workers' paradise was right in front of them. If they only seized the moment.

They even invented a weird economic theory called modern monetary theory (MMT)—the idea that the United States government could spend, borrow, tax, print money, regulate to almost no end. The politicians also seized the extraordinary power to almost entirely shut down the engines of the economy—as happened in many blue Democratic states in 2020. MMT enthusiasts said that as long as America remained toe global economic superpower and as long as the dollar retained its status as the global reserve currency, we had nothing to worry about from the Rocky- Mountain-high levels of debt. It was all practically FREE!

It was also fool's gold. What is the old life lesson: if something sounds too good to be true, it probably is. Bills, after all, have to be paid. Debts have to be repaid. (If not, we could all run up our credit cards with no regard to how we would pay up.) Borrowing against your assets can't go on forever, or you will lose everything. Can a nation like the US go bankrupt? Biden seems hell- bent on finding out. Go back to the Roman Empire (and every great kingdom throughout history) and fiscal chaos, insurmountable debts, and all the public corruption that inevitably goes with it follows. Then the empire falls under its own weight of public indebtedness, a tax regime that robs the workers and producers who create the national wealth, and…SNAP, the system goes bust almost overnight.

History is replete with such dramatic turning points that no one saw coming. One day the Berlin Wall was separating the Iron Curtain countries of the Soviet Union from the free world, and the next, it was gone. One day in 1999 it appeared that tech stocks would never collapse. Then they did and the economy tanked.

Then came the housing market meltdown in 2008–09. We should remember how almost overnight some of America's great and iconic companies and banks went belly up in a matter of days when the financial crisis hit. Here's a partial sample to bring back bad memories:

- Countrywide Mortgage Company $40 billion
- Bear Stearns $22 billion
- Fannie Mae $1 trillion
- Freddie Mac $1 trillion
- Merrill Lynch $440 billion
- AIG $100 billion
- Lehman Brothers $1 billion
- Wachovia National Bank $15 billion
- Lloyd's of London $40 billion
- UBS $59 billion
- IndyMac Bank $15 billion
- MF Global $43 billion

And many, many more.

Have we already forgotten the carnage from this financial Armageddon? One week these companies were sailing on the seas of Champagne and the winds of caviar. The next they were extinct. Then there were the Ponzi scheme artists like Bernie Madoff who went to jail after stealing billions from his patrons and investors. No one bothered to look under the hood to see whether there were real investments behind the frothy returns. It was all going so well. What you don't know can't hurt you.

Until it all crashed. Thousands of Americans lost their life savings to the fraudster. As some investors saw their net worth crumble to the ground, some even committed suicide—jumping out of the windows of Wall Street towers, reminiscent of what happened during the 1930s stock market crash.

One looks back at the financial bubble and the fraud that went on and we wonder…how could smart people (by that, I mean, us) be SO stupid. If something is unsustainable, it REALLY DOES stop. We, through an era of easy-money policy at the Federal Reserve Board, pipelined trillions of dollars like helium into a circus balloon. Home values doubled in many areas. The federal regulators at the Securities Exchange Commission, the FTC, the FDIC, the CFTC, and the inspector generals and federal auditors, and private auditors, and nearly everyone else partied like it was 1999, to borrow a phrase from Prince. It reminds one of the famous Jack Nicholson rant in the courtroom in *A Few Good Men*: "You want the truth? You can't handle the truth!"

Amazingly, few people went to jail. Almost no one in government lost their jobs. All but a few were caught with their pants down. Ignorance was anything but bliss. The same people who said the chances of a housing crisis and a collapse of the mortgage insurer, Fannie Mae, were "one in a million," were even rewarded with cushy jobs to clean up the mess. The losses were in the trillions of dollars. The blameless—the little guy—took a giant hit. Unemployment soared, as did poverty and homelessness. It took nearly a decade to dig out of the wreckage.

But this was all child's play compared to the financial tumult that we are facing under Biden and the progressive left.

IS THIS TIME DIFFERENT?

We have learned—or rather, we SHOULD have learned—that, as Milton Friedman taught us: there is no such thing as a free lunch.

But that is what Biden and the progressives are offering. A $6 trillion free lunch that allegedly doesn't need to EVER be paid for. What is proposed makes the New Deal, the Great Society, Obamacare, and even World War II spending look like chump change.

It's a story that we have seen again and again and again and again…and it does not have a happy ending. Our current $21 trillion of publicly held debt will nearly double to $40 trillion in ten years, then double again in the next decade.

The purpose of this book is to pull the five-alarm fire signal. This isn't a fire drill.

The historical trends provided here are found almost nowhere else. We had to go through archived data and publications to find the numbers and the trends from earlier times. This nation REALLY was founded on the principles of limited government and individual initiative and hard work and self-reliance.

The progressives have managed to turn common sense and basic laws of economics on their heads:

Here's a few of the nonsequitors, we are hearing with more and more regularity:

- Defunding the police will reduce crime.

- Raising taxes on investments will get America to invest more.

- Borrowing $4.5 trillion is necessary to stop inflation.

- Paying people up to $50,000 in unemployment and welfare benefits not to work will create more jobs.

- Decapitating the American fossil fuels industry will stop climate change even as China and India and other nations produce and consume more fossil fuels.

- Allowing biological males to compete in sports with biological females is a smart way to advance women's sports.

- Preventing new pipelines in the United States will stop climate change; but greenlighting pipelines in other nations will not hurt the planet.

- Printing more money doesn't cause inflation.

- Allowing Americans not to pay rent for eighteen months will help solve the affordable-housing shortage.

- Defunding charter schools, education scholarships, and vouchers that benefit minorities the most is a good way to fight racism.

- Forcing American workers to join a union and pay union dues against their will is the best way to help workers.

- Giving Amtrak another $50 billion from taxpayers even though every route it operates manages to lose money—and has for fifty years—is a good transportation "investment."

- Forcing Americans who sacrificed to pay off their student loan debts to now pay more taxes to pay off the student loans of the deadbeats who haven't is fair and equitable.

- Rewarding public schools whose doors have been shut for the past eighteen months with $100 billion more money is a good education policy.

- Stopping construction of a border wall that is 80 percent completed is a smart way to protect our border from terrorists, drug runners, and criminals.

- Giving the Biden administration $4.5 trillion more money to spend is justified because they did such a professional job with the evacuation of Afghanistan.

- Building 10,000 electric charging stations around the country so that Americans with $100,000 Teslas can recharge the batteries for free is a good way to reduce income inequality.

- Forcing the red states that kept their economies operating during the pandemic and kept their unemployment rates low to pay for a bailout of blue states that shutdown and have high unemployment rates is fair and equitable.

- Borrowing an additional $5 trillion over the next decade is the best way to help our children and grandchildren.

I could go on and on, but you get the point. This is what is passing as sound economic thinking in Washington these days.

Tooth Fairy Economics

The point of this book is NOT to argue that government borrowing is evil and always unproductive.

Sometimes it is quite appropriate for governments to borrow to finance long-term benefits to society. It is unquestionably appropriate to borrow to finance a war (as FDR did to win World War II and Reagan did to win the Cold War). It is also appropriate investments that raise the long term living standard and growth path of the economy. We would gladly borrow to finance the short-term transition costs to a flat tax. Within a decade at most, those costs would be recouped by much faster growth of the economy and for generations to come (as long as the low-rate flat tax remained in place), the growth dividend would multiply, making our kids and grandkids much richer than they otherwise would be. Dale Jorgenson, a Harvard economist, has estimated that the discounted present value of a flat-tax-type of shift from the current tax code would be close to $6 trillion. That is a windfall that we could and should be very willing to borrow to capture.

I also would gladly borrow (especially at today's very low interest rates) to finance the one-time transition costs to a fully funded and personally controlled and owned retirement system as a replacement for pay-as-you-go social security. With normal rates of return in the market, today's young workers and their children would retire with pension benefits more than double what they are expected to receive under the current benefit formula—and that assumes no changes to the program that are likely to happen and likely make a bad deal for our children even worse. This, too, would make future generations much richer, and the borrowing costs now to finance that transition would be offset by the lower government pension obligations in the future. And even the increase in federal borrowing would have no negative crowding impact on private investment, because every dollar of additional government borrowing for the next twenty years would be offset by an additional dollar of private savings stashed in the personal accounts. The national savings rate would be completely unaffected.

It is also true that some government spending has a positive economic return. Government plays an important role in the economy. Roads, schools, the judiciary, regulations, defense, and helping those in need come quickly to mind. Few dispute the benefits well-run government confers on society.

But with the Biden "stimulus" spending, most of the money doesn't fit into this category. Democrats on Capitol Hill argue that even funding for food stamps and unemployment insurance (which essentially pay people for working as little as possible), is a positive for the economy. But in the real world—in the U.S. and around the globe—runaway government spending has in most cases been—not a remedy for our weak economy but a contributing cause of our current malaise.

If you believe, as we do, that the macro economy is the sum total of all of its micro parts—that is to say, what every American contributes to the production of the economy—then the theory of stimulus spending really doesn't make much sense. Boiled down to its essence, the Biden economic plan enables the government to take additional resources above and beyond what it would otherwise take from one group of people (usually the people who produced the resources) and then gives those additional resources to another group of people (often to nonworkers and nonproducers). The qualification for receiving Biden's redistribution money is often the absence of work or income. Quite simply, government taxing more people who work and then giving more money to people who don't work is a surefire recipe for less work, less output, and more unemployment.

Then there is the fantasy declared by the progressives that government spending has a "multiplier effect." What does this mean? Princeton economist Alan Blinder once succinctly described the theory by writing that public sector spending causes a "multiplier effect; that is, output increases by a multiple of the original change in spending that caused it."

How big is that "multiplier?" The Biden team is predicting that every dollar of its "infrastructure bill" will yield up to $1.30 in benefits to the economy. Some in the Biden administration say that $1 of spending can lead to $1.50 and even $2 of economic benefit. Like fairy dust, the money gets spent over and over and ricochets from one store to another throughout the economy, enriching everyone who comes in contact with that single dollar. Under this model, the opposite is also true: cutting the government budget translates into vanishing jobs. By definition: government spending creates jobs. End of story.

And yet the notion that additional spending is a "stimulus" ignores such a basic accounting reality. Every check written has an offsetting debit. Government cannot claim resources until some private worker or business has produced them. That is why it is a self-evident truth that for every additional government dollar spent there is an additional private dollar taken. All the stimulus to the spending recipients is matched on a dollar-for-dollar basis every minute of every day by a depressant placed on the people who pay for these transfers. In an economy, the total income effects of additional government spending always sum to zero.

But the substitution or price effects of stimulus spending are almost always negative for all parties. The transfer recipient has found a way to get paid without working, which makes not working more attractive, and the transfer payer gets paid less for working, once again lowering his incentive to work. These substitution effects make less work relatively more attractive than working for both payers and receivers.

To believe otherwise is about as foolhardy as to believe in the tooth fairy.

Until Debt Do Us Part

This book is in part a history lesson. I present data from as far back as the birth of our nation in the late 18th century and throughout the nearly 250 years since. The historical data is instructive because it demonstrates how lean and efficient our government was in the early days of the Republic. Unless otherwise indicated, all of the data and charts are adjusted for inflation. Even still, the borrowing and spending envisioned is more than all of the wars, pandemics, natural disasters, and economic depressions our nation has faced—COMBINED.

Some of the somber findings:

- Federal spending will eclipse 50 percent of GDP

- The national debt will exceed $100 trillion

- The national debt will rise to 300 percent of our GDP

- Tax rates will have to rise to 50 percent on all economic activity and on all Americans to pay off this debt

- The average child born today will, by adulthood, have a more than $500,000 share of the national debt that they will be responsible for paying off

- Interest payments will consume one quarter to one third of all federal spending. That is, only at most seventy-five cents of every tax dollar will pay for government services. The other twenty-five cents will go toward paying off debt from previous generations.

Figure i-1

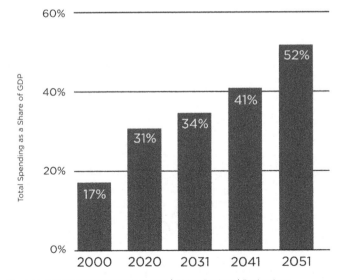

Under Biden Plan Government Becomes Larger Than Private Sector

Federal Spending as a Share of GDP with Biden Plan

In 2020 dollars

Sources: usgovernmentspending.com | Biden Budget | Projections

Figure i-2

Federal Debt Will Exceed Three Times Our GDP

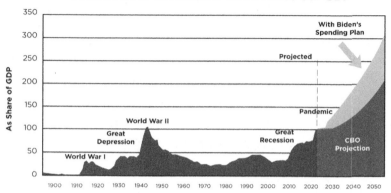

Sources: WH Historical Tables | Biden Budget Request | Projections

Figure i-3

The Financial Burden We Are Placing On Our Children

Debt Per Child in 2019 Dollars

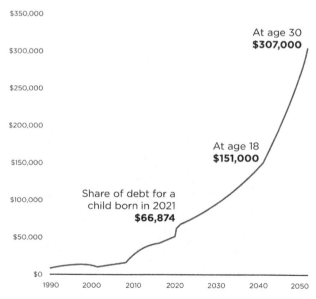

Sources: Census Bureau | White House Historical Tables | Biden Budget | Projections

Is this the gift that we want to bestow to our children? The Americans Dream is that every generation leaves the next one better off. Not more indebted.

This economic philosophy of government everlasting and almighty has been tried multiple times by great empires throughout history. It has always had an unhappy and even a catastrophic ending.

There is an old joke about a man whose home is underwater from hurricane flooding. On the first day a trooper comes in his squad car to assist him out of his home to safe land. He stands there in the front door with the water up to his belt buckle and says, "I don't need your help. The Lord will save me."

Two days later the rains keep coming and now the whole first floor of his home is flooded. The troopers come in a boat and tell him to hop in and they will take him to safety. He leans out the second floor window and shouts: "Go away, the Lord will save me."

Sure enough two days later the water is so high that the old man is forced to sit on the roof of his home. The Coast Guard brings a helicopter, which hovers over his home that is near to being swept away by the rising tides of water. They lower a rope and tell him to grab it and come aboard. He snuffs and says: "I keep telling you that don't need your help because the Lord will save me"

They shake their heads in disbelief and fly away.

That night the tide is so strong the poor gentleman is swept away in a swirl of flood water and he drowns.

When he gets up to heaven, he approaches the Lord, and he is dismayed. "Lord, I trusted in you to save me and you didn't."

The Lord shakes His head in wonder and looks down on him and says: "My son, I sent a squad car, then a boat, then a helicopter."

Let us not make that mistake. Let's rescue our country from a food of debt, taxes, and government spending that will be our undoing.

And let us hope that the old adage is true that Americans always manage to get it right after we try every other alternative.

Chapter 1
THE ROAD TO NATIONAL BANKRUPTCY

The system of bureaucratic despotism, elaborated finally under Diocletian and Constantine, produced a tragedy in the truest sense, such a history has seldom exhibited; in which, by an inexorable fate, the claims of fanciful omnipotence ended in a humiliating paralysis of administration; in which determined effort to remedy social evils only aggravated them until it became unendurable; in which the best intentions of the central power were, generation after generation, mocked and defeated by irresistible laws of human nature...

—Roman Society in the Last Century of the Western Empire by Samuel Dill, page 281

As we drift toward the abyss, I propose an interim measure: abolition of the word billions and trillions, words far too friendly to convey the magnitude of the sums they are meant to denote. Politicians, in particular, should be forced to say "thousand million" for "billion," and thousand, thousand million for the flip "trillion." It is a linguistic crime that the easy two syllable "trillion," hitched to a number like 4, should be permitted to express a debt that, had William the Conqueror begun saving for it in 1066 at the rate of $1 million a day, would still be unpaid today.

—Charles Krauthammer, "Tilting at the Deficit," *The Washington Post*, April 17, 1992

In recent decades we have seen the arrogance and expansion of government in every aspect of our lives.

Joe Biden has brought America to the very edge of a financial apocalypse that could make the disastrous 2008 market crash—with trillions of dollars of losses in stock, home values, lifetime savings, and business failures—look like a day in the park. I hope and pray I am wrong and that we will right the ship before we hit the iceberg.

But the capture of power by our government during, and in the aftermath of, the COVID-19 pandemic has been unprecedented in American history. As we document in this book, normally, in the aftermath of a crisis like this pandemic, we halt the spending and debt stampede, begin cutting back on government, and reverse the tide of debt.

- That was true after Revolutionary War

- That was true after the Civil War

- That was true after World War I

- That was true after the Great Depression and World War II

- That was true after the end of the Cold War

- That was true after 9/11

- That was true after the Financial Crisis of 2008–09

Figure 1-1

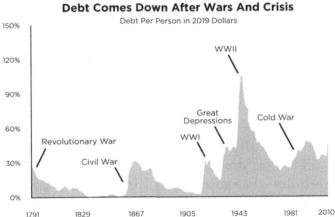

But now we are doing the opposite. The *Figures* below show that the amount of new spending and debt that Biden and the Democrats have proposed is greater than the amount (adjusted for inflation) spent to deal with every crisis from the Revolutionary War to the victory in World War II.

Figure 1-2

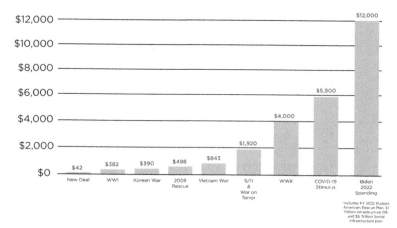

Biden Spending: Most Expensive in U.S. History

*Includes FY 2022 Budget, American Rescue Plan, $1 Trillion Infrastructure Bill, and $5 Trillion Social Infrastructure plan

Nothing was more degrading of our constitutional rights as the federal, state, and local response to the COVID-19 pandemic with governments shutting down businesses, schools (public and private), churches, stores, restaurants, parks, businesses, and passing out trillions of dollars of taxpayer money to special interest groups, imposing curfews, and stay-at-home orders. This was the first time in American history that the federal government felt empowered to quarantine even healthy people—and even those who were not in danger of the virus.

This was also the first time in history—even including wartime—that government spending reached 50 percent of our GDP. That means that government consumed and spent more than all of the resources of every private worker and business in America. Of course, government doesn't produce things. It can only spend a dollar when it takes a dollar from the private sector via borrowing or printing money. Much of this spending is justified on the premise that government reduces inequalities and inequities in our society. Even more prevalent nowadays is the idea of government spending as a "stimulus" to the economy.

Figure 1-3

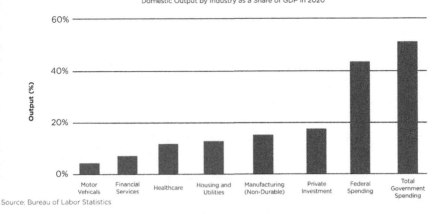

Government Is America's Largest Industry
Domestic Output by Industry as a Share of GDP in 2020

Source: Bureau of Labor Statistics

Of course, as a political matter, anytime government takes from Peter and gives to Paul, as the old saying goes, the politicians can always count on the support of Paul. But where is the evidence that government spending is a stimulant to anything but government itself? We have ample evidence from history that more government spending makes countries poorer over time, not richer. If that was not the case, then the Soviet Union would have won the Cold War. Cuba would be an island paradise. Socialist Europe would be richer than the United States.

This is not an argument for no government. But the evidence is incontrovertible that economic freedom—limited government, free trade, low tax rates, property rights, rule of law, human rights—is highly associated with economic prosperity. Economic freedom is also highly correlated with higher income standards of the poorest in a society. It is also associated with better health, better education, and a cleaner environment.

Figure 1-4

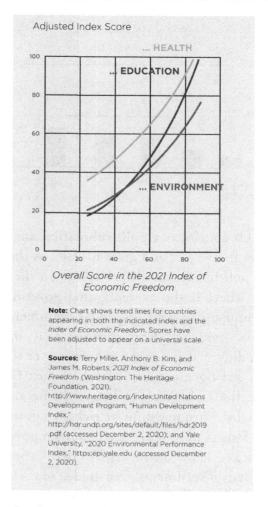

More Economic Freedom Also Means Better ...

Adjusted Index Score

... HEALTH

... EDUCATION

... ENVIRONMENT

Overall Score in the 2021 Index of Economic Freedom

Note: Chart shows trend lines for countries appearing in both the indicated index and the *Index of Economic Freedom*. Scores have been adjusted to appear on a universal scale.

Sources: Terry Miller, Anthony B. Kim, and James M. Roberts, *2021 Index of Economic Freedom* (Washington: The Heritage Foundation, 2021). http://www.heritage.org/index;United Nations Development Program, "Human Development Index," http://hdr.undp.org/sites/default/files/hdr2019.pdf (accessed December 2, 2020); and Yale University, "2020 Environmental Performance Index," https:epi.yale.edu (accessed December 2, 2020).

As we describe later in this book, "government as stimulus" has been a failed theory for more than one hundred years. The expansion of government under Herbert Hoover, one of America's worst presidents, and then under FDR's New Deal, which doubled the size of government in the 1930s, left America with a decade of double-digit unemployment and economic misery. During World War II, the government vastly expanded to defeat fascism. But this didn't create prosperity. This was a clear and present danger to the national security of the nation, but the Japanese and Germans didn't create improvement in the living standards of Americans any more than COVID-19 made America richer. Americans spent less on private consumption in the war years than they did during the Roaring '20s.

The expenditures, and the power grab that went with it during the pandemic of 2020, may have been justified (though I am highly skeptical). However, just as I and others feared and predicted, government is not surrendering the powers that it grabbed during the height of the crisis.

"A Crisis Is a Terrible Thing to Waste"

Barack Obama's chief of staff, Rahm Emmanuel, famously declared these words at the height of the 2008–09 financial crisis. For those who want bigger government, crises are opportunities to grab more power and ask citizens to surrender their freedoms.

Normally, when a crisis is over, government starts to shrink back in size, but as Robert Higgs taught in his famous book *Crisis and Leviathan*, government rarely recedes to its previous levels. It ratchets up in size. This is what happened in the years following World War II when government spending fell from 48 percent of GDP in 1945 to less than 20 percent of GDP by 1950.

But what is unique and worrisome about the environment we live in now is that, with the health pandemic crisis over thanks to the rapid development of vaccines—a private sector triumph—government isn't shrinking. Many agencies are actually accelerating.

Exhibit A is President Biden's release of his Fiscal Year 2022 budget blueprint, a plan that calls for the first $6 trillion budget in U.S. history and a $3.6 trillion tax hike; the largest tax increase in American history.

Figure 1-5

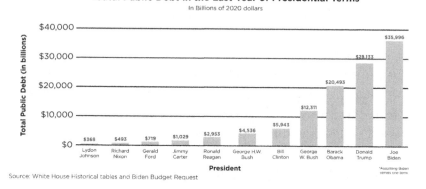

Toatal Public Debt in the Last Year of Presidential Terms
In Billions of 2020 dollars

Source: White House Historical tables and Biden Budget Request

In Biden's America, Everyone Is Entitled to Everything

Even the *Washington Post* once acknowledged in an editorial that in a democracy, "everyone can't be entitled to everyone else's money."

Well, they may have had that wrong, because Joe Biden is supersizing the entitlement state of America at a pace that makes LBJ's Great Society initiatives seem like a fiscal bargain. By the way, that was the infamous "War on Poverty" that spent more than $5 trillion over twenty-five years. As the old saying goes, we fought a war on poverty, and poverty won.

But here we go again. Biden already has spent $1.9 trillion on social welfare programs—ranging from unemployment benefits, free healthcare, more generous food stamps, rental assistance, and more money for schools and state governments. Now he wants to add to that a $3.5 trillion "social infrastructure bill" (this is the new term for "welfare") that includes all sorts of new entitlements, such as universal and fully subsidized daycare and pre-kindergarten, as well as free community college and student loan forgiveness for kids who went to Harvard. Democrats are also debating whether to make the $300 a week "temporary" bonus unemployment benefits permanent. That way no one will ever have to work.

Most dangerous of all is the planned expansions of Medicare and Medicaid. These programs already have a long-term deficit of more than $55 trillion, according to the watchdog group Truth in Accounting.

So naturally Biden and the Dems want to put more passengers on this fiscal Titanic.

The Medicare plan would provide a whole array of new benefits like vision, hearing, and dental care, all paid for by taxpayers. This at a time when Medicare trustees warn that Medicare's Part A Trust Fund is likely to run dry by about 2026, and possibly as early 2024. Seniors should be up in arms over this raid on the Medicare Trust Fund.

By the way, Congress already dipped into Medicare's reserves to help fund the COVID-19 bailout efforts in March of 2021.

David Jonas, a former staffer for Barack Obama, recently spilled the beans in a tweet about the Democrats' scheme here. He says "the politics here are near perfect" because "Medicare expansions are forever." He's right, of course. Once you start giving Americans free things, it's a near political impossibility to take them away. This is the insidious nature of the entitlement cancer cells.

The Dems also want to provide new bribes to citizens of red states to sign up for free Medicaid benefits. This program too is financially flimsy, and so, when Obamacare was created, many red states wisely refused to take the bribe of free money from Washington because they saw the new programs would puncture holes in their state budgets. So now, Democrats in Congress want to offer new subsidies under Medicaid for residents of the twelve states—such as Florida, Georgia, and Missouri—that opted not to widen their Medicaid benefits. They are calling these "Medicaid look-alike programs" to be administered by the feds.

Readers may be amazed that politicians continue to expand Medicare, Medicaid, Obamacare subsidies, and the like because twelve years ago we were told that the trillion-dollar Affordable Care Act (Obamacare) was going to provide universal coverage for everyone. But we keep spending hundreds of billions of tax dollars, and all we hear is how many millions of Americans still lack health coverage. Maybe that is because all the money the feds spend on healthcare is making the whole system way more expensive.

Oh, and if all of this isn't enough, the Democrats want to make the $300 a month payments per child a permanent fixture of the budget. This is on top of the $2,000 per person we sent out early in 2021.

University of Chicago economist Casey Mulligan and I recently published a study sponsored by the Committee to Unleash Prosperity that found that thanks to Biden's new welfare-state expansions, families can get up to $100,000 in government benefits (tax free) without anyone working a single hour all year!

The government will feed you, pay your rent, educate you, take care of your kids and your grandparents, pay for your college and day care, pay you if you aren't working, pay for your healthcare, and your toothbrush, and your internet hookup, and soon free iPhones (that should be an entitlement, shouldn't it?).

The real mystery about this new cradle-to-grave entitlement state is why Americans still bother to work at all.

To Infinity and Beyond

In his budget message President Biden said that his budget proposal "is a statement of values that define our Nation at its best."[1] God forbid. What it reflects is an administration that has lost touch with financial reality. It is based on a fraudulent economic fad theory called "Modern Monetary Theory," which posits that with low interest rates, the federal government can borrow and borrow for years on end without negative effects. It is a "fool's gold" concept that threatens to bankrupt our nation.

I believe that the rosy assumptions behind this budget scenario are highly unlikely, and other budget watchdog groups, such as the Committee for a Responsible Federal Budget, agree. Given the lower growth that is associated with more government spending, the amount of new spending and debt, and the historical record of entitlement programs growing at about double their expected size, suggests that passing the Biden budget on top of the already gloomy fiscal scenario will mean a debt binge over the next twenty years that could exceed $50 trillion.

Federal spending alone will double over twenty years to more than $10 trillion. (That's thirteen zeroes!) How do you like socialism now?

---

1   Budget of the U.S. Government Fiscal Year 2022, Office of Management and Budget, https://www.whitehouse.gov/wp-content/uploads/2021/05/budget_fy22.pdf

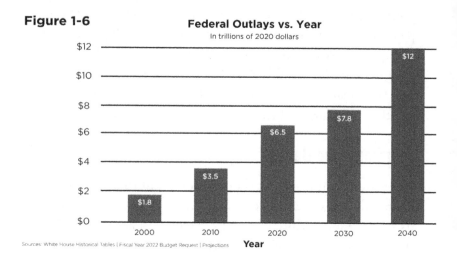

Figure 1-6

Federal Outlays vs. Year

In trillions of 2020 dollars

Sources: White House Historical Tables | Fiscal Year 2022 Budget Request | Projections **Year**

The Biden budget priorities demonstrate that this administration is clearly trying to be the bridge between the quasi-socialist government we already have, and a true socialist regime of government that constantly expands faster than the private sector. Don't take it from me, take it from Joe Biden's budget message to Congress:

> **"The Budget is built around a fundamental understanding of how our economy works and why, for too long and for too many, it has not. It is a Budget that reflects the fact that trickle-down economics has never worked, and that the best way to grow our economy is not from the top down, but from the bottom up and the middle out."**

Biden's chief economist Brian Deese has called for billions of dollars of corporate welfare spending (what we call "aid to dependent corporations") and he justifies the surge in handouts by saying: "The idea of an open, free-market economy ignores the reality that China and other countries are playing by a different set of rules.

Strategic public investment [corporate welfare] to shelter and grow champion industries is a reality of the 21st-century economy." He wants a new government-directed national industrial policy to replace free enterprise and private capital markets.

Great. Now politicians are going to pick industry winners and losers. Milton Friedman taught us the fallacy of this logic many years ago by reminding us: "You never fight a government subsidy with a government subsidy."

Biden also says that his goal is to relegitimize government as a positive force for good and a fountain of goodies to be distributed—er, redistributed—from rich to poor, and from private businesses and workers to federal agencies, bureaucrats, and dependents on government.

This is all code for more government, more taxes, and more regulations. As I write these words, President Biden's administration is trying to get the prairie chicken listed as an endangered species (its population is growing, not shrinking) so that thousands of acres of oil and gas drilling lands can be put off limits. One small and seemingly inconsequential new Interior Department dictate could shut down tens of billions of dollars of oil production in the Permian Basin in Texas.

Biden and the progressives that have taken over the Democratic party are so enthralled with the power of government that they now want to count his trillions of dollars of debt-financed spending as having a positive impact on the economy. Among the so-called "pay-fors" in the infrastructure bill is supposed revenues to be generated from the "macroeconomic impact of infrastructure investment." So now we are using dynamic scoring to count government spending as a net plus to the economy? Apparently, in this new-age budget scoring, the more money the government takes from private families and businesses and wastes on itself, the faster the economy grows.

Senate Minority Leader Mitch McConnell is right when he attacks the spending and taxes in the Biden plan. "So far this administration has recommended we spend 7 trillion additional dollars this year. That would be more than we spent in adjusted inflation dollars to win World War II… So they have huge spending desire and…a great desire to add in $3.6 trillion in additional taxes on top of it."[2]

To be perfectly honest, Republicans have hardly been better as guardians of the public fisc. The spending and borrowing disease in Washington is, alas, clearly bipartisan. Republicans just want to spend a little less. So, for example, when Democrats call for $2 trillion on public works, Republicans respond that they only want to spend $1.2 trillion.

CAN BIG GOVERNMENT SAVE US?

President George Washington famously warned "government is a fearsome master." Abraham Lincoln called freedom "the last, best hope on earth." Ronald Reagan told voters: "Government is not the solution to our problem; government is the problem." Donald Trump rallied his voters with the promise to "drain the swamp" in Washington, D.C.

President Biden's philosophy "build back better," by contrast, is predicated on the belief that an omnipotent and enlarged government will be our savior. According to this progressive philosophy, government is not "a necessary

---

2 "Biden Budget to Run $1.8 Trillion Deficit to Finance Spending Plans," *Public Broadcasting Service News*, May 27, 2021, https://www.pbs.org/newshour/economy/biden-budget-to-run-1-8-trillion-deficit-to-finance-spending-plans.

evil" but a positive force for a fairer, more compassionate, and more prosperous nation. Our benevolent Uncle Sam can solve nearly every problem, from ending poverty to reversing racism, to putting a chicken in every pot, to changing the temperature of the planet, and stopping the rise of the oceans.

The White House proposes a $4.1 trillion spending increase for what he calls the American Jobs Plan and the American Families Plan. That is on top of the $1.9 trillion spending plan passed in his first one hundred days. Amazingly, Biden has proposed six times as much spending as Barack Obama did to deal with the financial crisis.

Figure 1-7

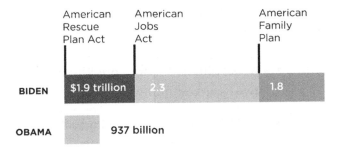

Biden Spent 5x More in First 100 Days Than Obama

Source: The Wallstreet Journal

All of this is reflected in his legislative ambitions. The American Jobs Plan is a $2.6 trillion infrastructure plan that is aimed at everything except true infrastructure—roads and bridges. Here are some highlights of the American Jobs Plan:

- $621 billion in Green New Deal transportation, including $174 billion for electric vehicle subsidies

- $590 billion in Green New Deal manufacturing and job training, including $35 billion for climate change research

- $400 billion for clean-energy tax credits

- $100 billion for broadband subsidies

- $30 billion for 75,000 more IRS agents

- $10 billion for urban transit systems (with almost no riders), Amtrak, and high-speed rail systems to nowhere

The American Families Plan is a $1.8 trillion welfare plan aimed at making American families more dependent on federal government programs. Here are some highlights of the American Families Plan:

- $506 billion for free pre-kindergarten and free two-year community college

- $495 billion for "families and children," including childcare benefits, free meals, and food stamps

- $855 billion in expanded tax credits, including $125 billion for the Earned-Income Tax Credit

The expansion of welfare benefits under Biden—extra unemployment benefits, rental assistance, food stamp expansions, student-loan forgiveness, $3,000 credits per child, $2,000 per family, and expanded Obamacare subsidies would mean that, in these states, a family of four could collect the wage and salary equivalent of a $100,000 annual salary—without either spouse working a single hour. For more than half of households, welfare paid more than work! We all believe in a temporary safety net for people who lose their jobs, but the safety net has turned into a hammock.

Figure 1-8

Wage And Salary Equivalent Of Maximum Benefits On An Annualized Basis
Two Unemployed Parents and Two Children

State/District	Annualized Payments	Hourly Wage Equivalent
Massachusetts	$147,198	$37
Washington	$138,095	$35
New Jersey	$136,403	$34
Minnesota	$132,644	$33
Connecticut	$129,656	$32
Oregon	$125,441	$31
Hawaii	$123,654	$31
Pennsylvania	$121,911	$30
Illinois	$121,363	$30
Rhode Island	$119,208	$30
Colorado	$117,568	$29
Kentucky	$115,482	$29
Maine	$115,312	$29
Vermont	$112,049	$28
Kansas	$109,271	$27
California	$109,062	$27
New York	$108,859	$27
New Mexico	$107,541	$27
Nevada	$106,131	$27
DC	$101,176	$25
Delaware	$98,698	$25
Virginia	$97,771	$24
Wisconsin	$91,678	$23
Michigan	$90,123	$23
North Carolina	$90,047	$23
Louisiana	$82,044	$21

Source: Committee to Unleash Prosperity

All of these governmental expansions will force Americans to pay more in taxes. The Congressional Budget Office expects that over the 2021–2030 period, the entitlement trust funds will face a deficit of $2.3 trillion.[3] Yet President Biden is calling for a new 3.8 percent Medicare tax and a 12.4 percent payroll tax increase for millions of Americans to pay for programs that we cannot afford and have no authority to enact at the federal level.[4]

What Ever Happened to Checks and Balances?

President Biden's budget steers us toward the financial doomsday scenario that I have been warning about for decades. His budget will take our country straight into a financial wreck where the young and the old will be forced to pay for the consequences of irresponsible politicians. As we will show later in this book, even if this Congress rejects all of Biden's precocious spending ideas, we still face a mountain of debt in front of us simply from the massive government transfer programs that are already baked into the federal cake and that are exacerbated by the aging of the 75 million baby boomers.

So the Titanic is headed to the iceberg. Biden just wants to speed up the ship!

What makes our current predicament scary in the extreme is that the guard rails against runaway spending that were established in the Constitution, and 250 years

---

3 The Outlook for Major Federal Trust Funds: 2020 to 2030, Congressional Budget Office, September 2020, https://www.cbo.gov/publication/56541.

4 Tax Proposals of President-Elect Biden and Other Prominent Democrats, *The National Law Review,* January 13, 2021, https://www.natlawreview.com/article/tax-proposals-president-elect-biden-and-other-prominent-democrats.

of safeguards built into our system of representative government, are now being circumvented or ignored.

In the past, what has slowed down such audacious power grabs by political parties in America has been the ingenious system of checks and balances set up by our founding fathers who warned of, and protected against, the dangers of concentrating power in the hands of a few. This is why, of course, we have three branches of government. This is why we have three levels of government: cities, states, and the federal government. This is why we have staggered terms for our elected officials. This is why we have two, not one, houses of Congress. This is why conventions like the Senate filibuster were set up requiring a supermajority to pass legislation.

The founding fathers wanted to make it difficult for Congress to grow government by changing our laws in the "passions of the moment." The president was given a veto power to repel what he believed to be bad or unjust legislation. The courts were set up, as James Madison put it, to serve as a "bulwark of our liberties."

When one of the most popular presidents in modern times, Franklin Roosevelt, tried to pack the Supreme Court in the early 1930s to push through his New Deal legislation (his so-called "switch in time to save nine" justices) the nation revolted against this naked power play. His coup attempt against the courts failed miserably.

But now, the progressives who have seized control of the presidency and Congress are trying to pull off the most audacious power play in American history. This is why Biden has also proposed a power sweep by:

- Packing the Supreme Court

- Ending the sixty-vote filibuster in the Senate

- Adding Washington, D.C., as a state to add two Democratic senators (the Constitution is clear that this would require a Constitutional Amendment)

- Changing voting rules, including an end to Voter ID laws

- Federalizing elections

- Repealing right-to-work laws in twenty-six states, which would mandate that workers join unions

- Ramming through budget laws (such as pay-as-you-go budgeting) to increase the size of government

- Using "crises" like "saving the planet from climate change" or reversing "racism" as an excuse to take away our rights to free speech, our rights of peaceful assembly, and our 9th and 10th amendment protections that say that all rights not specifically granted to the federal government are "reserved for the states and the people."

We saw the vast expansion of governmental power during the Obama administration, with $1 trillion stimulus bills, Obamacare's encroachment of the healthcare system, and repealing welfare reforms to allow more Americans to become wardens of the state.

Under Trump and the Pelosi–Schumer Congress, we saw unthinkable expansions of governmental power during the pandemic. As the chart below shows, government grew faster than any other single industry during the COVID-19 crisis. In 2020, government was the number-one growth industry in America—with the output and spending of the state outpacing the output of all 10 million private firms and 150 million workers for the first time in American history.

But these were supposed to be temporary spending bulges during a once-in-a-half-century pandemic. Trump's Operation Warp Speed cleared away governmental hurdles to allow our vibrant and innovative private drug and biotech firms to develop a life-saving vaccine. What the *New York Times* predicted would take "at least" two or three years, happened in 10 months. It was a miraculous achievement, and it happened, as do almost all great achievements, inventions, and breakthroughs, in the US of A.

Private enterprise pulled it off in record time: about 10 months. That was an extraordinary achievement and showed what can happen when government has the wisdom to step aside and let the free enterprise system combat our greatest threats.

The pandemic is over. The virus has been defeated. But much of the massive infrastructure of government used to win the war against COVID-19 not only remains in place, it also is being expanded at once-unfathomable levels. How predictable was this? As Reagan used to quip: "There is nothing on this earth that is immortal other than a government program."

During the Obama administration, coming out of the financial-housing crisis of 2008–09, the Democrats called for $1 trillion in fiscal "stimulus." The Biden Administration wants

$6 trillion in "stimulus." To help the unemployed during the Obama administration, Congress approved a bill to give unemployed workers a $25 a week supplement to unemployment benefits. Under Biden those benefits skyrocketed to $600-a-week bonus benefits.

I call what is going on in Washington the "Big Squeeze." Government is squeezing out the private sector by taking money from private producers, either through taxes, borrowing, or printing money, and commanding those benefits for redistributionist and socialistic dreams. That game plan of endless spending and debt has never had a happy ending anywhere in the world. That's why they dare not call it socialism. But that is what it is. Under the Biden spending plan, federal government spending would lurch to 50 percent of all national output over thirty years. Revenues are not the problem, as the chart shows. Spending is.

Figure 1-9

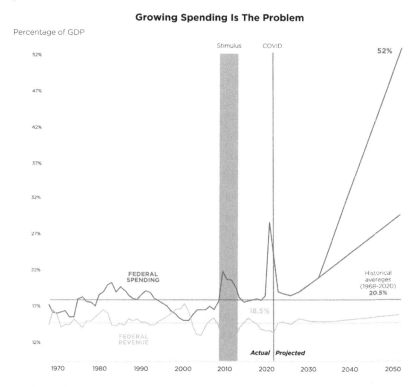

Growing Spending Is The Problem

Sources: CBO and OMB

It speaks volumes that the one avowed "social Democrat" in Congress, Bernie Sanders of Vermont, has fully praised the Biden agenda as containing nearly everything he wants. At what cost to our financial future and the future of freedom in the land of the free?

We are reminded of a YouTube video that shows a man in a black suit with a black tie who knocks on the door of a home, and a woman answers the door with two toddlers playing in the living room. He says to her: "Ma'am, we are here to collect your $150,000 worth of the national debt." She screams. "$150,000! I don't have $150,000!" The agent replies: "Ma'am, I wasn't talking to you. I was talking to those kids behind you."

Why Government Grows and Liberty Yields

Thomas Jefferson warned us that the natural course of events is for "government to expand and liberty to yield." He wisely advised us to be "forever vigilant" in protecting our freedoms.

Why have we abandoned his words of wisdom? How have we allowed this path to bankruptcy to happen in America—the land of the free?

Throughout history, nations and empires that have followed the financial course that we are now on have experienced the same progression. This cycle comes in three stages:

Stage 1: Tax and Spend. The demand for government spending begins to outpace incomes. Politicians attempt to pay for the mushrooming government expenses by continuously raising taxes. But they run head-first into an iron law of economics, which is that the higher tax rates are lifted, the less additional revenues they yield.

The tax and spend cycle also eventually collides with an iron law of politics: the electorate will tolerate higher taxes only up to a point. Then they revolt.

Stage 2: Borrow and Spend. When raising taxes to keep pace with rising expenditures becomes politically futile, politicians turn to borrowing. And borrowing from the public and foreigners is an attractive short-term fix. But lawmakers soon discover that increasingly heavy borrowing imposes its own financial constraints. The debts have to be continuously repaid with interest, which adds to already-voluminous expenditures. This creates a demand for still more revenues, creating a fiscal treadmill whereby the government must run faster and faster just to stay in place. Creditors become increasingly uneasy about the creditworthiness of the government and its commitments to honoring its rising debts. The politicians soon discover that financing government through borrowing is an exercise in frustration—like the greyhounds racing around the dog track, trying to chase the ever-elusive mechanical rabbit.

Stage 3: Inflate and Spend. With debts piling up and the cost of borrowing rising inexorably, government often turns to its third option to pay for uncontrolled spending: printing money. This inflation of the currency also carries with it an additional, short-term political benefit for government in that it not only raises revenues, it also reduces the real value of outstanding debt. Historically, however, inflation spirals out of control and degenerates into hyperinflation. Ultimately the nation begins to either make draconian and painful reductions in public services and benefits, or is dragged into the abyss of complete financial insolvency.

Are We Imitating the Losers?

Think of the fate of countless third-world countries that have experienced rampant inflation and a tailspin of the impoverishment of their citizens. I am speaking of nations like Argentina, Bolivia, and Brazil. In Argentina, a nation that had gained stature as one of the world's five wealthiest by the end of the first half of the twentieth century, massive public debts gave way to 500 and 600 percent inflation in the mid-1980s. These policies proved financially ruinous for the citizens of Argentina. The nation became so debt-plagued in the 1970s that the inflation raged at 1,000 percent and more. Living standards in Argentina plummeted by more than 20 percent in the 1980s. This once-proud economic superpower fell to virtual third-world status by the late 1980s thanks primarily to irresponsible government spending and lending behavior. It was only now, decades after the slide began, that Argentina abandoned statist policies, and showed signs of genuine economic revival.

Venezuela embraced "progressive" redistributionist policies under Hugo Chavez in the early 2000s, and the country nosedived into one of the worst depressions in modern history. A country that got rich off of massive oil reserves so impoverished its citizens that hungry masses started to eat animals in the zoos.

Or consider the more recent and tragic tale of Chile and think about what happened there...and the similarities to what is happening here in America.

Back in the 1970s, the nation of Chile embarked on one of the boldest sets of free market economic reforms in history. The government called in the Chicago Boys, as they were called, led by Milton Friedman and other University of Chicago free-market economists.

They were given a free hand to redesign the Chilean economic system with property rights, a low flat tax, privatization of the Social Security system, and deregulation of industries. In 1991 Friedman wrote that Chile now has "the three freedoms: economic freedom, political freedom, and human freedom. It will be interesting to see if they can keep it."

For four decades, the experiment worked better than anyone could have imagined. According to a study by economist Axel Kaiser for the Cato Institute: "Between 1975 and 2015 per capita income in Chile quadrupled to $23,000, the highest rate in Latin America (CNP 2016). As a result, from the early 1980s to 2014, poverty fell from 45 percent to 8 percent (CNP 2016)." Chile became one of the richest nations in South America. And it happened in three decades; an eye blink of history.

The Marxists and intellectual class of Latin America always hated the free-market reforms. They disparaged the Chicago Boys as "fascists," and spent decades attacking the policies (with the stooges in the American media echoing their protests) even as Chile was becoming the jewel of South America.

The Marxists invented a narrative of inequality; "the rich were getting richer and the poor were getting poorer;" and that capitalism is evil.

They infiltrated all of the cultural institutions of Chile: the media, the schools, the universities, the Catholic church, the arts, the unions, and even the corporate board rooms. They spread their poisonous creed of collectivism to the populace.

Does any of this sound familiar to our situation today?

Eventually, the leftists pulled off a political coup. In 2013, the left won the Chilean presidency. The free-market reforms were systematically replaced with "spread the wealth" platitudes. In October 2020 voters approved a rewrite of the Constitution, and now property rights and the rule of law are in danger.

Chile is now in economic freefall. The poor are getting crushed. The rich are pulling their money out of the country. They have arrived at "equality." Nearly everyone is suffering.

Meanwhile, back in America this cautionary tale is what our kids and college students—so enamored with socialism—should be learning in the classrooms. Fat chance. The left runs our schools now, too.

And what they have in mind is a sweeping economic transformation. The Biden administration is promising to help the middle class by passing our trillions of dollars of free money to citizens, and paying people more money for not working than for working. We will borrow trillions of dollars and pray that the Chinese continue to buy up our bonds and that our currency holds up.

A sock-it-to-the-rich tax increase is coming that will make the productive class and the job creators pay their "fair share" with tax rates of 50, and 60, and 70 percent.

Beware Modern Monetary Theory

How will the left pay for all its Olympic-record spending plans? Even Biden's massive tax hike would, at most, offset half the cost of the budget binge.

This is the last and most devious part of the left's plan to transform our free-market system to statism. The left-wing academics have brought to Washington a shiny new economic philosophy that the intellectuals and the political class is starting to embrace.

I am speaking of the absurd and dangerous theory called Modern Monetary Theory—something conjured up by a gang of leftist academics at second-rate universities. The theory postulates that a rich nation like the United States that has the status of world reserve currency (i.e., the dollar) can spend and borrow into the trillions of dollars as long as interest rates stay low and inflation does not ignite. But this is like saying that someone who jumps out of the 81st floor of a building is doing just fine up until the moment they crash into the concrete sidewalk.

It is hugely dispiriting that anyone would take seriously this "theory," which is equivalent to believing that the earth is flat. This is crackpot economics, but alas, there are many people in high levels of government today in the swamp of Washington who are following Modern Monetary Theory. That includes the man sitting in the Oval Office. His reckless fiscal policy will test the limits of federal borrowing and money printing.

It is hard to comprehend how our increasingly fat, flabby, and inefficient government will pass the stress test that we impose on banks and other financial institutions. The fiscal dam will burst, if we don't stop the rising tide of spending and borrowing and the "Don't Worry, Be Happy" ethic in Washington. But binges have painful hangovers.

The message of this book is that it is long past time that we started worrying. Houston—or rather, Washington—we have a problem.

Chapter 2

THE GOOSE THAT LAYS THE GOLDEN EGGS

The primary lesson of the 20th century is that communism and socialism are failures, and free markets are a success. Why then, do so many intellectuals believe that we need more socialism?

—Milton Friedman, 1998

We Americans are so used to sustained economic growth in per-capita production that we tend to take it for granted—not realizing how exceptional growth of this magnitude is on the scale of human history.

—Simon Kuznets

The biggest issue facing the planet over the next ten, twenty, and fifty years is not climate change—although protecting our environment is a critical objective.

By far the larger issue for the future of freedom, peace, and global prosperity is whether America will continue to be a world economic superpower—a status that the United States has held for almost a century now. We have had rivals for sure. Germany in the 1930s, the Soviet Union after World War II, then Japan in the 1970s and 1980s. And now, China.

The fundamental message of this book is that America didn't get rich by chance—though some say it was divine providence that guided the United States to freedom and prosperity. America got rich on the back of a free enterprise system that allowed economic opportunity, invention, entrepreneurship, and grit to create world-class businesses and products. It is not an accident that the most profitable companies in the world today—Amazon, Apple, Microsoft, Facebook, and Google—were all made in the USA.

China will only overtake us economically if we do ourselves in with unbridled government spending, debt, taxes, and a regulatory apparatus that strangles the life out of our enterprising spirit and impoverishes us.

How America Got Rich

For more than two centuries America has been a beacon of freedom for the rest of the world, and our primary role in the global economy has been to lead by example.

The history of the United States is a history of spectacular progress—in health, in wealth, in incomes, in affordability of goods and services, in leisure time, in education, and even improvements in the environment—perhaps unparalleled in all of human history. In fact, the advances have been so rapid that it's hard for Americans today to fully appreciate how far we have progressed in a very short time.

Throughout most of the 20th and early 21st centuries, the American economy has grown at a real rate of between 3 and 4 percent per year. *Since 1900, real incomes of American families have doubled roughly every thirty years. The idea of a shrinking middle class—or working class stagnation—is mostly a myth.* Throughout the 20th and 21st century, every generation of Americans has roughly succeeded in achieving a living standard that has been nearly twice that of their parents. Real per capita income has risen from about $3,000 in 1900 to over $59,000 today. *In just under one century, the standard of living in the United States has grown by nearly 9,500 percent.*

That is the per capita income, which could easily be thrown off by the presence of so many millionaires and billionaires among us. In a football stadium with 80,000 poor people that also includes Amazon founder Jeff Bezos, the per capita income will be very high. So what if we look at the median income in America—that is the households at the exact middle—half higher and half lower. That income rose to nearly $70,000 in 2019, which in most countries today would be considered rich.

Figure 2-1

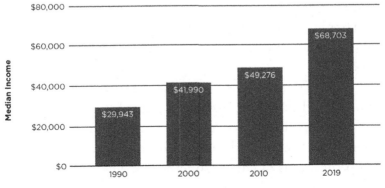

Median Income Continually Rises

Source: Census Bureau

One prominent example of the American productivity revolution has been the meteoric rise in the output of the American farmer. More than one hundred years ago, about half of the U.S. workforce was employed in agriculture and produced enough food for the 75 million Americans alive at that time. Now, less than 3 percent of Americans are farmers, and they not only feed themselves and the other 255 million of us, but also they feed tens of millions more around the globe. We produce roughly three times as much food on one third as much farmland with one third the workers as we did one hundred years ago. The United States is unquestionably the bread-basket of the world.

To fully appreciate this achievement, consider that throughout human history the primary struggle of nations has been to feed themselves. It is a testament to the economic miracle of the United States' capitalist system that, over the past several decades, our government's farm policy has been devoted to reducing food production in order to keep prices high and surpluses to a minimum. What a wonderful problem for a nation to have!

The digital revolution we are now living through is easily the single-greatest thrust forward in human progress in world history. The average smartphone today has more computing power than the early multimillion-dollar supercomputers used during World War II. The average smartphone has tens of thousands of times more computing power than was used to send the Apollo missions to the moon.

The shale energy revolution is another recent innovation bonanza that almost overnight tripled American oil and gas reserves. Instead of America running out of cheap and abundant energy, in the last twenty years, America has run into the status of energy superpower. The price of oil and gas plummeted and the U.S. became energy independent. New Biden rules restricting energy production in the U.S. threaten to pull the plug—literally and figuratively—on this bottomless well of energy.

The shale revolution is also an example of how we rely on the free enterprise system to find solutions to problems that once seemed irreversible. Thirty years ago, no one would have believed that America would become an exporter of energy, but that happened in early 2020.

Meanwhile, our material wealth is today far superior to what it was fifty and one hundred years ago and far superior to the level achieved by other nations of the world. In 1950 there were about thirty cars per one hundred persons; now, there are more than seventy-five. In 1950, telephone service reached just 2 percent of American homes versus 95 percent today, nearly half of which have cordless phones. In 1950 television was still a novelty. Today more than 90 percent of American households own at least one color TV.

Even households that are considered "poor" in the United States today are relatively well-off in their standard of living when compared to households of even thirty years ago and are rich compared to the average non-American. Poverty expert Robert Rector of the Heritage Foundation reports that the median household income of American living in 1960, after adjusting for inflation, was 10 percent lower than median expendity of Americans officially classified as poor today.

According the US census bureau:

- More than 78 percent of poor families have air conditioning

- More than 80 percent of poor families own a car

- More than 81 percent of poor families have a microwave oven

- More than 97 percent of the poor own a TV

- The average poor American household has twice the housing space as the average income Japanese household and four times the living space as the average Russian household

See the chart below:

Figure 2-2

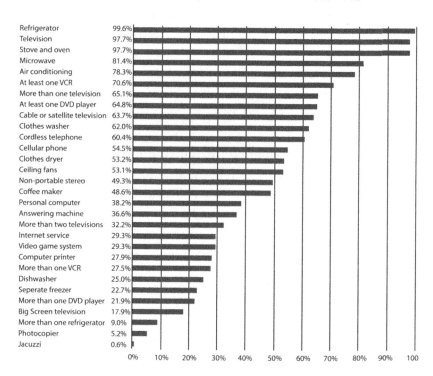

America's Poor are Doing Better Than Ever
Percentage Of Poor U.S. Households Which Have Various Amenities

Amenity	Percentage
Refrigerator	99.6%
Television	97.7%
Stove and oven	97.7%
Microwave	81.4%
Air conditioning	78.3%
At least one VCR	70.6%
More than one television	65.1%
At least one DVD player	64.8%
Cable or satellite television	63.7%
Clothes washer	62.0%
Cordless telephone	60.4%
Cellular phone	54.5%
Clothes dryer	53.2%
Ceiling fans	53.1%
Non-portable stereo	49.3%
Coffee maker	48.6%
Personal computer	38.2%
Answering machine	36.6%
More than two televisions	32.2%
Internet service	29.3%
Video game system	29.3%
Computer printer	27.9%
More than one VCR	27.5%
Dishwasher	25.0%
Seperate freezer	22.7%
More than one DVD player	21.9%
Big Screen television	17.9%
More than one refrigerator	9.0%
Photocopier	5.2%
Jacuzzi	0.6%

Data Collected From: U.S. Department of Energy, Residential Energy Consumption Survey, 2005

Source: The Heritage Foundation

There is much truth to the adage "if you have to be poor, America is a good place for it."

America's progress is not only evident in her economic accomplishments. Throughout history, life on earth for the vast majority of men and women has been, as Thomas Hobbes described the state of nature, "solitary, poor, nasty, brutish, and short." People seldom lived beyond the age of fifty. Children and their mothers routinely died at birth. Diseases, plagues, and famines were capable of wiping out half of a nation's population. The essence of the human struggle has been to preserve and lengthen life.

In the 20th and 21st centuries, this pattern changed dramatically. As shown in figure 2–3:

- In 1900, life expectancy in the US was 47

- In 1950, life expectancy was 68

- In 1992, life expectancy was 76

Figure 2-3   **Life Expectancy (from birth) in the United States, from 1960-2020***

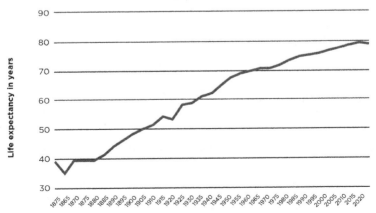

Sources: UN DESA; Gapminder

These longer life spans are the result of technological advances in farming, the launching of the era of modern medicine and its introduction of hundreds of new life-saving drugs (most of which were invented here in the United States), better diets, healthier lifestyles, and higher incomes.

An even more heartening triumph has been the rapid decline in infant mortality. A child born today is four times more likely to survive past their first year of life than a child born a hundred years ago. This dramatic decline in infant mortality, together with longer life expectancy, represents a stunning triumph over premature or early death in the United States. And we have exported this triumph to every corner of the globe, where similar but less dramatic trends are being recorded. In fact, it is precisely because babies are more likely to survive after they are born, and because people are living longer lives, that the American population has steadily climbed in this century. How foolish that many American intellectuals decry this trend rather than celebrate it.

None of this is intended to trivialize the plight of the less fortunate or to imply that there are no serious economic and social inequalities in the United States. The central point here is that few nations have succeeded in improving the living standard of their citizens as well as the United States in this century.

How America Grew Rich

Humanitarians often look around the world, seeing overwhelming and heartbreaking poverty, and wonder why so many people are poor. They ask the wrong question. The normal human condition throughout history has been for humans to be poor and to live at subsistence levels.

The question we ought to be asking is: why are there a few countries, most prominently the United States, that are rich? What is the formula for economic success and prosperity?

In the United States the formula has been astonishingly simple. It is the combination of freedom, free enterprise, and limited government. Or, as John F. Kennedy put it in his famous address before the Economics Club of New York in 1962, the growth of the American economy in the 20th century "demonstrates for all to see the power of freedom and the efficiency of free institutions."

More specifically, America's formula for economic success has included:

- Protection of private property rights

- Rewards for hard work, enterprise, and initiative

- Guarantees of basic political freedom and human rights, such as freedom of speech and religion

- Free trade of goods and services

- The relatively unrestrained immigration of energetic and productive people who impart economic energies on those already here

- A minimally burdensome and distortive tax system

- Establishment of constitutional protections against the unchecked expansion of government

- Personal freedom

All of this might be best summarized by Thomas Jefferson in his famous adage: "That government which governs best, governs least."

When other nations have adopted this formula of freedom and free enterprise, they have generally produced favorable results. After World War II, nations like Hong Kong, Taiwan, Singapore, Japan, and West Germany—to name a few—adopted free markets as their economic governing philosophy. Much of the rest of the world—including China, the Soviet Union, Cuba, North Korea, and others—moved toward socialism and communism.

The Soviet Union, of course, collapsed under its own weight of bureaucracy, tyranny, poverty, and despair. Khrushchev famously warned in the early 1960s after his trip to America that "we will bury you." In the end, we buried Russia, or it may be more accurate to say that the USSR buried itself. America, with our free enterprise system, grew three to four times richer than the average Russian living under Soviet oppression.

With our superior economic system, China became so poor under Maoism that tens of millions of the country's own citizens starved to death (and this horrific number might be even higher than the official statistics).

In the 1980s China shifted directions toward a more free enterprise system—albeit with tight government controls. The same was true of India. These countries did not become free market Meccas by any stretch of the imagination. But the direction was toward freer and more open markets. In these two countries, over thirty years, almost one billion people were moved out of abject poverty. We are skeptical that the statist interventions in the economy from the political leaders in Beijing will lead to a continuing economic acceleration—but it is still too early to tell when, and if, the China bubble bursts.

Economic Freedom Matters

An age-old question that historians and economists have long-pondered is why do some countries grow richer than others? Some say it is natural resources; others say it is geographical advantage. Still others claim ethnicity or the religion of a country; others claim the amount of foreign aid that a nation receives, the quality of education, and so on.

Yes, those can all be important factors in why one group of people economically advance faster than others. But countries like Hong Kong and Singapore have grown very rich with almost no natural resources. America is about the most ethnically diverse country on the earth—homogenizing many ethnicities and cultures into one melting pot—so it is doubtful that cultural factors or DNA are dominant. Countries that receive a lot of foreign aid from other nations tend to grow more slowly, not faster than others. As many poor African countries have proven, charity is a temporary lift but not a permanent one.

The factor that seems to be overriding all others is economic and human freedom. Each year, the Heritage Foundation publishes an index of economic freedom based on many of the factors that we discuss in this book. These include:

- Low tax rates

- Free trade

- Protection of private property

- Rule of law (no gangster capitalism)

- Limited government

- Light regulation

It should not be too surprising that Heritage's index proves fairly conclusively that economic freedom is very highly correlated with economic success and higher living standards for all. By virtue of the fact that we live in a nation that is mostly economically free (though we are moving in the opposite direction of late), an American has about five to ten times the income of someone living in a nation that has very little economic freedom—such as North Korea, Cuba, Zimbabwe, or Venezuela.

Figure 2-4

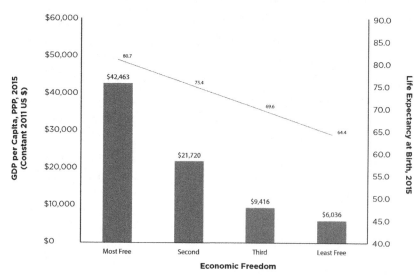

Free Countries Are Wealthier And Healthier

Source: Cato Institute and Fraser Institute, Economic Freedom of the World, 2017.

Cuba, by the way, is a very visible example of a country that went from being fairly prosperous in the 1950s with a highly educated and productive workforce, and modern amenities—like cars, trucks, air conditioning, paved roads, etc.—that moved toward socialism/communism in the early 1960s under the tyrant, Fidel Castro. Freedom was torn asunder, and under the dictatorial and brutish policies of the pro-Soviet Cuban regime, Cuba's living standards plummeted. The nation, over the next half century, became the place that time forgot. All that worked in the country were things like buildings and cars and factories built before 1960. Cuba has all the advantages a nation could want—it could and should be the Hong Kong of the Western Hemisphere, and yet Cubans still risk their lives and all that they have to get out.

What is far more surprising is that other factors associated with a just and stable society beyond just GDP growth are also tied to economic freedom. For example, nations with free markets also show substantial socioeconomic progress; they have better health outcomes, longer life spans, and more opportunity. The poor do better in these nations than in countries that "share the wealth." In other words, "economic justice" and "fairness" is far more prevalent in free enterprise nations than in autocratic countries where wealth is tied to political power and connections, not productivity, hard work, and entrepreneurship.

But what about the state of the environment? We are told that capitalist systems are raping the planet and emitting massive pollution into the air and water. Capitalism is thought to be bad for the health of our planet. We are told we need a massive regulatory state to stop greenhouse gas emissions to save the planet.

Yes, of course, responsible environmental regulation is critical. You don't have the right to pollute the river and send your toxic waste onto my property. Sound environmental regulation is consistent with a free-market system.

But it is also true that countries that operate under free market capitalism have a much better record of cleaning the air and the water than nations that are socialist and communist. For example, America's water and air is cleaner today than at any time in the last one hundred years—at least. This is also partly a result of the truism that when a country gets richer, it puts a much higher value on a clean environment with clean air and wide open spaces.

Meanwhile, the two nations that have polluted the planet the most over the past century are…Russia and China. Both have had totalitarian leaders that care not a whit about the environment.

Free market capitalism will save the planet. Socialism/communism will destroy it. That is the enduring lesson of history.

Killing the Goose that Lays the Golden Eggs

This brings us back to the point Milton Friedman made that we quoted at the start of this chapter. If free enterprise makes us richer, freer, more educated, and creates a fairer society, why are we so enamored with socialism? It is one of life's great mysteries. Clearly the move toward more socialism and government control that we are unfortunately seeing in America today is being driven by the intellectual classes. Professors, philosophers, the clergy, the media, Hollywood, and the education establishment; the chattering classes. Those who talk and think, but do little in the way of producing.

There is an old twist to the Marxist line that "religion is the opium of the masses." It goes like this: "Marxism is the opium of the intellectuals." And it is true. We have real-life Marxists teaching Marxism on college campuses today, which makes about as much sense as celebrating the life of Mao or Pol Pot.

This intellectual fascination with socialism and big government has infected the political class and it explains why our government now is nearly 50 percent of everything we produce.

Nobel Prize winning economist James M. Buchanan once described the free enterprise system in America as "the goose that lays the golden eggs." In recent years many Americans have begun to wonder whether the goose is still fertile.

In fact, a recent public opinion poll asked respondents to compare the next generation's standard of living with the current standard of living.

Figure 2-5

2017 Poll: Americans Fear Children Will Be Worse Off

*When children today in our country grow up they will be
____ financially than their parents*

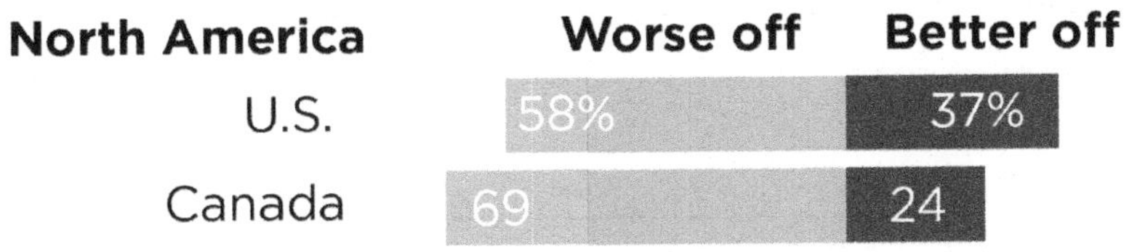

North America	Worse off	Better off
U.S.	58%	37%
Canada	69	24

Source: Pew Research *modified for presentation purposes*

In the U.S. 37 percent predicted that the next generation's living standard would be "better," and 58 percent said it would be "worse." In other words, most Americans fear we are going backward.

The level of apprehension is understandable. Our recent economic performance has been highly disappointing. We have lived through two extreme traumas already in the 21st century. The first was the housing bubble bursting which caused a horrific financial meltdown in 2008–09. Then COVID-19 and the massive growth of government spending, debt, and power over our lives plunged America into even further despair.

The legacy of these crises—which in both cases was in no small part a result of governmental incompetence—has been a national debt that now costs every household $150,000, and soon that number will be $300,000.

Figure 2-6

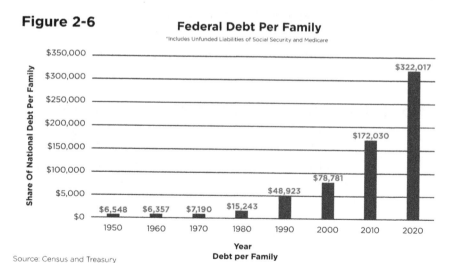

Federal Debt Per Family

*Includes Unfunded Liabilities of Social Security and Medicare

Source: Census and Treasury

The Tax Burden: in 1950, taxes took one of every twelve dollars of the American worker's income. In 2020, taxes took one of every three dollars from American workers. In 1990 taxes consumed well over one of every three dollars of worker income.

Government Bureaucracy: In 1900, 4 percent of the American workforce was employed by the government. In 1950, that number had risen to 10 percent of the American workforce. In 2020, 15 percent of Americans—one out of every seven workers—got their paycheck from the government.

The Rise of the Welfare State: Real total social welfare expenditures exploded from $10 billion in 1990 to $130 billion in 1950 to $1 trillion in 1992. That's more than the GDP of all but a handful of countries. Today, one of every nine Americans collects food stamps. In New York City, one of every seven residents is on welfare.

The Crushing Burden of Debt: The national debt now stands at a towering $29 trillion. This represents a $322,017 debt burden for every family in the United States.

The Regulatory Stranglehold: In 1935 there were 4,000 pages of regulations listed in the Federal Register. Today there are 65,000 pages of such regulations. The economic cost of complying with federal regulations is now estimated to be at least $1.9 trillion per year. Economic regulation has the impact of a tax on every American worker. The amount of this tax is estimated to be about $350,000 for every household in the US each year.

A Trillion Here and a Trillion There

Some 80 years ago Senator Everett Dirksen described how Capitol Hill politicians throw around money: "a billion here, and a billion there, and pretty soon you're talking about real money." If he were alive today, he would have to amend what he said and put it like this: "a trillion here, and a trillion there, and pretty soon you're talking about real money."

Part of the problem with our supersized federal budget is that the numbers get so large, we can't even comprehend the magnitude or scale of our government take over. We all know a million dollars is a lot of money. But how much is a billion? How much is a trillion?

Behavioral psychology tells us that when something becomes so large that we can't conceive it—like the size of our galaxy—it becomes meaningless. We blank it out. If I told you, I lost $10,000, you would probably think: "oh my God, that is a lot of money to lose!" If I told you the government lost $10 billion, you would have no frame of reference. This may actually seem conceptually like a smaller amount than the $10,000 you can envision.

So let us help you, the reader, conceive of how much money our $6 trillion budget is.

Ignoring gravity for a moment, say you were to have an unlimited supply of $5 bills and you decided to stack them one after another until you hit $6 trillion. Believe it or not, your imaginary stack of bills would hit the Moon before amounting to $6 trillion. Let that sink for a second, a stack of $5 bills so tall that it reaches the Moon, would still not be enough money to cover this insane budget.

The federal budget is now about $6 trillion, and the state and local governments spend roughly just under

$3 trillion, bringing the total public expenditures to $8 trillion–$9 trillion. Meanwhile, the federal debt has reached more than $21 trillion. The war on poverty has cost almost $15 trillion, according to the Cato Institute. Total federal liabilities are more than $80 trillion.

The problem is that one trillion is an unfathomably large number. Four trillion is simply four times an unfathomably large number. This explains why the release of the federal budget is not met with public outrage but rather with a national shrug of dazed incomprehension.

Even the politicians themselves have become anesthetized to the large amounts of money they dole out each year and the fiscal devastation this causes. When President Clinton released his $1.42 trillion budget for 1992 ($50-billion increase) legislators applauded the president for being frugal and tightfisted inside the Washington Beltway. Later Congress passed a new anticrime, social welfare program entitled "an ounce of prevention." Its price tag: $1.3 billion. Yes, a billion three is now considered an ounce on Capitol Hill.

So, to help arouse some genuine ire, outrage, and understanding, let's try to put a human face on a trillion dollars. A trillion dollars is $1,000,000,000,000. If you're counting, that's twelve zeroes to the left of the decimal point. Here's one way to think about how much that is: a trillion is one-thousand-million dollars. Most Americans are lucky to earn $1 million in their lifetimes.

How does the size of the federal budget compare to the size of the economies of other nations? Figure 2-7 shows that the federal government spends more than all of the people in Germany. Our government is larger than the entire GDP of Australia and Spain combined.

Figure 2-7   **U.S. Budget Larger than Most Countries' Entire GDP**

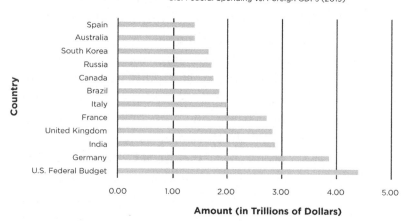

U.S. Federal Spending vs. Foreign GDPs (2019)

Source: Organisation for Economic Co-operation and Development | Biden Budget

One of the highest paid workers in America today is Los Angeles Lakers superstar, Lebron James, who reportedly earns about $42 million a season in salary and tens of millions more with endorsements. He is rich beyond our wildest imaginations. But he would have to play 25,000 seasons before he earned $1 trillion. It would take 100,000 millionaires like LeBron James— standing-room only Rose Bowls full—to pay for one day of all federal, state and local spending in the US.

Here's an interesting experiment: what if we were to try to pay off the $22 trillion national debt by having Congress put one dollar every second into a special debt buydown account? How many years would it take to pay off the debt? One million seconds is about two days. One billion seconds is roughly thirty-two years. But one trillion seconds is almost 32,000 years. So if Congress put dollar bills into this account for about the next 130,000 years—roughly the amount of time that has passed since the ice age—the present debt would be paid off.

Even if we were to require Congress to put $1,000 a second into this debt reduction account, it would still take well over 1,000 years to pay down the debt. Translation: thanks to our spendthrift politicians, the federal government will be in the red for a long, long time.

Try this one on for size: imagine a train of fifty-foot boxcars crammed with one-dollar bills. How long would the train have to be to carry the one-and-a-half trillion dollars Congress spends each year? About $65 million can be stuffed into a train boxcar. The train would have to be 250 miles long to carry enough dollar bills to balance the federal budget. In other words, to balance the budget, you would need a train full of dollar bills that covers the entire Northeast corridor from Washington, through Baltimore, Delaware, Philadelphia, New Jersey, and into New York City.

Former Reagan budget director Jim Miller uses this analogy: imagine a military jet flying at the speed of sound, reeling out a roll of dollar bills behind it. It would have to fly for fourteen years before it reeled out one trillion bills.

If you read every word in the *New York Times* every day for a year, you would have to read nearly 30 million words. But you would have to do this for about 300,000 years before you would have read one trillion words. (Imagine the drudgery of having to read every word of the *Times* for more than 30,000 years!)

If you laid one dollar bills end to end, could you make a chain that stretches to the Moon with one trillion? No problem. In fact, if you laid one trillion dollars end to end it would stretch from Earth to the Moon and back again 200 times before you ran out of dollar bills! One trillion dollars would stretch nearly from the Earth to the Sun.

Finally, with the $2.5 trillion that local, state, and federal governments spend each year, you could purchase all of the farmland in the United States, plus all of the assets of the Fortune 100 companies.

In sum, one trillion is a lot of railroad cars, newspapers, trips to the Moon, a lot of farmland, and most importantly, a lot of our hard-earned tax dollars to send to Washington—no matter how you stack it.

A $10 Trillion Federal Budget? Still the Land of the Free?

Americans have long viewed the government as a benign force that protects the public welfare. That may have been true one hundred or even fifty years ago, but today's government is so large and meddlesome that it is undermining public welfare. More than any hostile foreign nation, more than any criminal, more than any natural disaster, our own United States government today is the single-greatest threat to our economic security and basic freedoms.

Our economic problem is not that the American formula for success—the formula that created a run of economic progress unmatched in human history—does not work anymore. It's that the formula has been abandoned, and our rights and freedom have been usurped in favor of new political doctrines of greed, envy, dependency, entitlement, and paternalism.

Washington has slain the goose that lays the golden eggs.

Chapter 3

LIBERTY YIELDS AND GOVERNMENT GROWS

*Government is like fire, a dangerous servant
and a fearful master.*

—George Washington

The fire that the father of our country warned of has turned into a raging forest fire.

It is worth noting that Washington wasn't the only prominent founding father who worried about runaway government. Published in 1785, Benjamin Franklin's *The Way to Wealth*—a collection of writings from *Poor Richard's Almanac*—warned of a nation or a family racking up massive unpaid debts. "But what madness must it be to run in debt for these superfluities!" Franklin wrote. "But, ah, think what you do when you run in debt; you give to another power over your liberty."

A man notorious for his sensible frugality, Franklin, and the other Founding Fathers for that matter, would be flabbergasted by the current state of our nation's finances. Staring down $28 trillion in national debt and nearly $87 trillion in total debt, we continue to spend extravagantly as if the future will never come. In the 21st century, annual budgets of approximately $4, $5, and even $6 trillion have become routine. Instead of addressing the looming visage of fiscal insolvency, the federal government continues to appropriate record sums for superfluities.

How We Got Here

In 1800, when the nation's capital was moved from Philadelphia to Washington, D.C., all of the paperwork and records of the United States government were packed into twelve boxes and then transported the one hundred and fifty miles to Washington in a horse and buggy. That was truly an era of lean and efficient government. In the early years of the Republic, government bore no resemblance to the colossal empire it has evolved into today. In 1800, the federal government employed three thousand people and had a budget of less than $1 million or about ($250 million in today's dollars).

Today the U.S. federal government with its budget of $6 trillion spends $411 million every hour. The government workforce is closer to 18 million employees collecting a paycheck provided by taxpayers.

Since its frugal beginnings, the U.S. federal government has come to subsidize everything from Belgian endive research to maple syrup production to the advertising of commercial brand names like Sunkist in Europe and Japan, to rental assistance payments to people who don't pay their rent on time, to self-esteem classes, midnight basketball leagues, and the construction of local swimming pools. Not long before his death, Supreme Court Justice Antonin Scalia—in a moment of high drama before the Supreme Court, during oral arguments involving the application of the interstate commerce clause of the Constitution—pressed the Solicitor General to name a single activity or program that our modern-day Congress might undertake that would fall outside the bounds of the Constitution. The stunned attorney for the government could not think of one.

A Rulebook for Government

But wait! The U. S. Constitution is more than anything else a rulebook to restrict the powers of government. Its guiding principle is the idea that an unrestrained ruling class can be a source of corruptive power and ultimate tyranny. Washington's responsibilities were confined to a few enumerated powers involving mainly national security and public safety. In the realm of domestic affairs, the Founders sought to guarantee that federal interference in the daily lives of citizens would be strictly limited. They also wanted to make sure that the minimal government role in the domestic economy would be financed and delivered at the state and local levels. The enumerated powers of the federal government to spend money are defined in the Constitution under Article I, Section 8. These powers include the right to "establish Post Offices and post roads; raise and support Armies; provide and maintain a Navy; declare War…" and to conduct a few other activities related mostly to national defense.

No matter how long one searches, it is impossible to find in the Constitution any language that authorizes at least 90 percent of the civilian programs that Congress crams into the federal budget today.

The federal government has no authority to pay money to farmers—let alone to select aid on the basis of race—run the healthcare industry, impose wage and price controls, provide job training, subsidize electric cars, lend money to businesses and foreign governments, or build parking garages and local courthouses. The Founders did not create a Department of Commerce, a Department of Education, or a Department of Housing and Urban Development. This was no oversight; they did not believe that government was authorized to establish such agencies.

Recognizing the propensity of governments to expand, and, as Thomas Jefferson put it, for "liberty to yield," the Founders added the Bill of Rights to the Constitution as an extra layer of protection. The government was never supposed to grow so large that it could trample on the personal and economic liberties of American citizens.

The 10th Amendment to the Constitution states clearly and unambiguously: "The powers not delegated to the United States by the Constitution…are reserved to the States respectively, or to the people." In other words, if the Constitution doesn't specifically permit the federal government to do something, then it doesn't have the right to do it. The very first appropriations bill passed by Congress in the late 18th century consisted of one hundred and eleven words—not pages, mind you, words. The main expenditures were for the military, including $137,000 for "defraying the expenses" of the Department of War, $190,000 for retiring the debt from the Revolutionary War, and $95,000 for "paying the pensions to invalids." As for domestic activities, $216,000 was appropriated. As constitutional scholar Roger Pilon of the Cato Institute has documented, even expenditures for the most charitable of purposes were routinely spurned as illegitimate. In 1794, James Madison wrote disapprovingly of a $15,000 appropriation for French refugees: "I cannot undertake to lay my finger on that article of the Constitution which granted a right to Congress of expending, on objects of benevolence, the money of their constituents."

Those were the days.

To get a sense of how far we have strayed from our Constitutional principles, consider this famous story of Davy Crockett, who was elected to the House of Representatives from the state of Tennessee in 1826. During his first term of office, a $10,000 relief bill for the widow of a naval officer was proposed. Colonel Crockett rose in stern opposition and gave the following eloquent and successful rebuttal:

> **We must not permit our respect for the dead or our sympathy for the living to lead us into an act of injustice to the balance of the living. I will not attempt to prove that Congress has no power to appropriate this money as an act of charity. Every member upon this floor knows it. We have the right as individuals to give away as much of our own money as we please in charity; but as members of Congress we have no right to appropriate a dollar of the public money.**

With a few notable exceptions during the nineteenth century, Congress, the president, and the courts remained faithful to the letter and spirit of the Constitution with regard to government spending. As economic historian Robert Higgs noted in *Crisis and Leviathan*, until the twentieth century, "government did little of much consequence or expense" other than running the military. The total expenditures for the federal budget confirm this assessment. Even as late as 1925, the federal government was still spending just 4 percent of national output.

Abandoning the Constitution

In 1932, Charles Warren, a former assistant attorney general, wrote a popular book titled *Congress as Santa Claus*. "If a law to donate aid to any farmer or cattleman who has had poor crops or lost his cattle comes within the meaning of the phrase 'to provide for the General Welfare of the United States,'" he argued, "why should not similar gifts be made to grocers, shopkeepers, miners, and other businessmen who have made losses through financial depression, or to wage earners out of employment? Why is not their prosperity equally within the purview of the General Welfare?" Of course, we now know Congress's answer: all of these things are in the "general welfare."

This is why we now have unemployment compensation, the Small Business Administration, food stamps, fifty-two job training programs, and so on.

In the five years prior to World War I, total federal outlays averaged 2 percent of GDP. In the five years after the war, they averaged 5 percent of GDP. In the years prior to that war, the top income tax rate was 7 percent. During the war, the tax rate shot up to 70 percent, which was reduced afterward, but only to 24 percent— or more than three times higher than it had originally been. Government regulations of the private economy also proliferate during times of war and often remain in force afterward.

Robert Higgs notes that during World War I, the federal government nationalized the railroads and the telephone lines, requisitioned all ships over 2,500 tons, and regulated food and commodity prices. The Lever Act of 1917 gave the government the power to regulate the price and production of food, fuels, beverages and distilled spirits. It is entirely plausible that, without the war, America would never have suffered through the failed experiment of Prohibition. World War II was also the genesis of many modern-day government intrusions—which were and still are of dubious constitutionality. These include wage and price controls, conscription (which lasted until the 1970s), rent control in large cities, and, worst of all, federal income tax withholding. In the post-World War II era, Congress has often relied on a war theme to extend its authority into domestic life. Lyndon Johnson launched the modern welfare state in the 1960s when he declared a "war on poverty." In the early 1970s, Richard Nixon imposed across-the-board wage and price controls—the ultimate in government command and control—as a means of winning the "inflation war." In the late 1970s, Jimmy Carter sought to enact a national energy policy with gas rationing and other draconian measures by pleading that the oil crisis had become the "moral equivalent of war."

But the emergencies of the last dozen years have stuck a stake through the heart of our once-cherished constitutional restrictions on government. After the financial crisis of 2007–08, George W. Bush agreed to the once-unthinkable trillion-dollar expenditures to bail out businesses, banks (the Troubled Asset Relief Program [TARP]), car companies, financial service firms, and union pensions. Bush memorably defended these programs by saying we had to "abandon the free market system to preserve it."

Barack Obama came into office and doubled down on the Bush government interventions. The Democrats single-handedly passed a nearly $1 trillion "stimulus" plan that failed to revive the economy. The first three years of the Obama presidency gave America the weakest recovery from a recession since the Great Depression. Only when Congress started to restrain government spending did the economy start a slow road to recovery.

When the COVID-19 crisis hit in 2020, government asserted uncharted assaults on personal liberty and grabbed control of the purse strings with more trillions of dollars of aid to businesses, families, state and local governments, churches; and nearly everyone and everything became dependent on government. As mentioned previously, government reached 50 percent of our GDP. All these programs were supposed to be temporary.

But now we have President Biden in the White House. And even though the pandemic was winding down when Biden entered office, he and his progressive cronies in Congress would not let this crisis go to waste. He has proposed more than $7.5 trillion in spending. That is a ridiculously far cry from the first budget of the United States, which called for $750,000 in spending. In fact, it is ten million times the amount of spending.

Everyone Is Entitled to Everyone Else's Money

Since World War II, the U.S. government has spent increasingly more of its citizens' money year over year. Figure 3-1 shows the dramatic expansion just in the past century of the federal budget. This doesn't even include the $6.8 trillion spent in 2020 to deal with the COVID-19 crisis or the Biden multitrillion dollar spending blowout in 2021 and 2022.

Figure 3-1

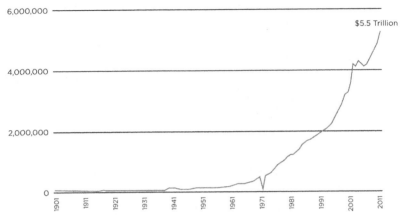

Federal Outlays, 1901-2019 (Millions of 2021 Dollars)

Source: usgovernmentspending.com

The small spikes seen in the 1910s and the 1940s of course are attributable to the first and second World Wars, but the continual increases since the latter of those two present a different pattern. Since the years between the two World Wars, the federal government has systematically eroded the Constitutional protections that our founders enshrined against runaway government and set record after record for massive government intervention into the private sector.

This new level of intervention is highlighted by the two spikes in federal outlays around 2008 and 2020. The first spike correlates to the federal government's heavy-handed response to the financial crisis of 2007–08 in which Congress provided "stimulus" funding that was, at the time, record-breaking. The second spike is still occurring. Since spring 2020, Congress has appropriated nearly $6 trillion in an attempt to address the recession caused by COVID-19 lockdowns.

To make matters worse, President Biden's budget request for FY 2022 calls for over $6 trillion in federal outlays. With the worst of COVID-19 presumably behind us, President Biden's proposed budget would slightly decrease federal outlays only because of the expiration of temporary COVID-19-related programs like the Paycheck Protection Program. Instead, President Biden would have federal outlays significantly exceed pre-COVID-19 levels by dramatically increasing spending on existing social programs coupled with costly new social programs.

In particular, President Biden's so-called "Build Back Better" plan, which encompasses the American Jobs Plan and American Families Plan, would dramatically increase the size and scope of the federal government. Proposals like free four-year higher education, universal preschool, costly investments in unproven technologies like electric vehicles, and promises to "redress historic inequities" in every aspect of American life threaten to balloon federal spending to emergency COVID-19 levels indefinitely.

This general trend toward fiscal insolvency is also born out per capita. As figure 3-2 shows, federal outlays are rapidly approaching $18,000 per person. As we continue to spend recklessly and are forced to finance future debt, that number will continue to grow.

- The federal government spent $43 per person in 1800

- The federal government spent $225 per person in 1900

- The federal government spent $9,574 per person in 2000

- The federal government spent $20,633 per person in 2020

Figure 3-2

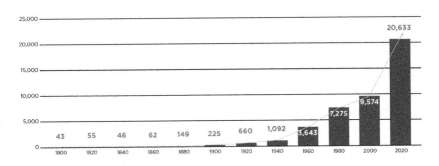

Per Capita Federal Outlays, 1800-2020 (2021 Dollars)

Source: usgovernmentspending.com

Another way to view the total costs of the federal government is to compare federal spending to the size of the American economy. When we examine federal outlays as a share of GDP, as is shown in Figure 3-3, it is clear that, although our economy continues to grow rapidly, the growth in federal spending far outpaces economic growth. Since 1900, federal spending as a share of GDP has grown from a mere 3 percent to 31 percent in 2020. When comparing Figures 3-1 and 3-3, we see that the noticeable decrease in federal outlays as a share of GDP in 2000 is mostly attributable to the high growth spurred by the "dot-com boom" that peaked around 2000.

- In 1900, the federal government consumed less than 5 percent of total output

- In 1960, the federal government consumed just over 15 percent of total output

- In 2020, the federal government consumed more than 30 percent of total output

Figure 3-3

Federal Government Growing Faster Than The Economy

Federal Outlays As A Share Of GDP, 1900-2020 (2020 Dollars)

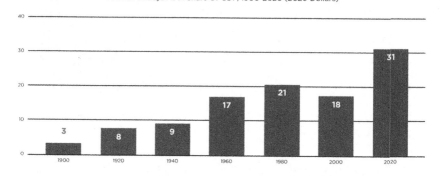

Sources: usgovernmentspending.com | Projections

National Defense

Some might reasonably assume that America's seemingly endless interventions in the Middle East are one of the primary drivers of increased federal spending. On the contrary, the estimated $6.4 trillion we have spent on post-9/11 wars is merely a drop in the bucket compared to the rest of the federal budget. As Figure 3-4 shows, defense discretionary spending has consistently been taking up less and less of the total budget. While total expenditures on national defense have predictably increased in recent decades, increases in mandatory and nondefense discretionary spending have outpaced increases in defense spending.

- Defense spending was nearly 50 percent of federal outlays in 1962

- Defense spending constituted 24 percent of federal outlays in 1990

- Defense spending constituted only 11 percent of federal outlays in 2020, which was an all-time low

Figure 3-4

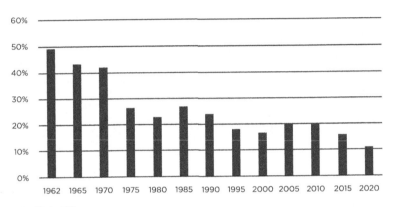

Defense Spending Continues to Fall

Defense Discretionary Spending Share Of The Federal Budget, 1962-2020

Source: Congressional Budget Office

Furthermore, as Figure 3-5 illustrates, the clear driver of federal spending is domestic programs, not defense spending. In fact, especially in the past decade, spending on nondefense programs (both discretionary and mandatory as a percentage of GDP) has dramatically increased, while spending on defense has decreased. No matter one's beliefs on the proper level of defense spending, it is dishonest to blame the explosion in federal spending on the defense budget. It is simply not true.

Figure 3-5

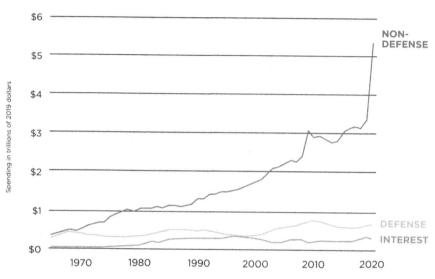

Defense Spending Is Not The Problem
Non-Defense Spending Spree

Data Collected from: OMB, CBO, Federal Reserve Bank of St. Louis.

Source: The Heritage Foundation

Healthcare

One significant driver of this trend is the increased federal intrusion in the health and healthcare marketplaces. No other part of the federal budget has grown so rapidly over such a short duration of time. Over the last thirty years, federal outlays for health have increased six times from roughly $100 billion in 1990 to roughly $600 billion in 2019. Figure 3-6 demonstrates this increase.

Figure 3-6

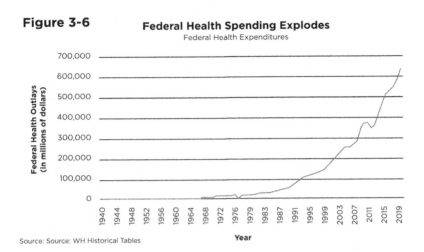

Federal Health Spending Explodes
Federal Health Expenditures

Source: Source: WH Historical Tables

In recent years, this growth has been induced primarily by increased costs associated with the Affordable Care Act, also known as Obamacare. In 2012, the Congressional Budget Office estimated the gross additional costs of Obamacare to be $1.5 trillion between 2012 and 2021. These costs were mostly consumed by Medicaid and the Children's Health Insurance Program (CHIP), with the remainder being comprised of tax credits and subsidies for health insurance on the public exchanges.

Looking at Medicaid on its own paints a similar picture. As shown in Figure 3-6, Medicaid spending has exploded in the last twenty years from just over $200 billion in 2000 to well over $600 billion in 2019. To put it another way, Medicaid expenditures are three times larger now than they were in 2000, and 116 times larger than they were in 1970.

Figure 3-7   **The Explosion In Medicaid Spending**

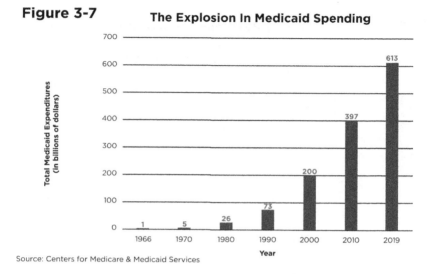

Source: Centers for Medicare & Medicaid Services

Education

From No Child Left Behind to Common Core, the American taxpayer has spent the last few decades continually pumping more funding into public education with little to show for it.

In the most recent international ranking by the Programme for International Student Assessment (PISA)— part of the Organisation for Economic Cooperation and Development (OECD)—the United States ranked 25th overall in educational achievement. Although we continue to spend luxuriously on our public schools, we clearly aren't getting much bang for our buck compared to our international peers. There are many reasons for this trend of lagging educational achievement, but, as Figure 3-7 demonstrates, more dollars do not necessarily correlate to higher test scores.

Figure 3-8

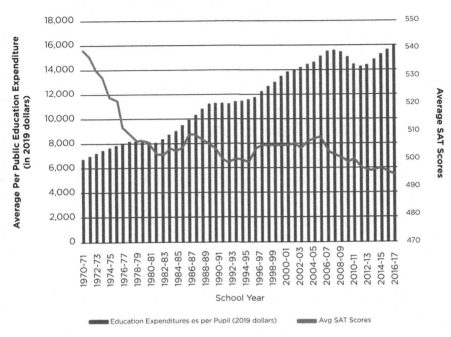

More Education Spending Leads To Worse Results
Per-Pupil Educational Expenditures vs. SAT Scores

Education Expenditures es per Pupil (2019 dollars)　　Avg SAT Scores

Sources: College Board | National Center for Education Statistics

Founded in 1978, the federal Department of Education (ED) was intended to support the education of America's students by coordinating and administering federal grants and other assistance programs. As its own mission statement makes clear, the intended goal of the ED is to "promote student achievement and preparation for global competitiveness by fostering educational excellence and ensuring equal access." Based on the data, clearly the ED is failing at its stated goal.

Since Jimmy Carter created the Department of Education, the federal government has spent $1 trillion on the schools. They have continually gotten worse. Perhaps we would do better for our children if the Department of Education didn't exist at all. By the way, the word "education" does not appear once in the Constitution, meaning such missions must be left to states and more appropriately local communities and families.

The Rise of the Welfare State

Any discussion of our fiscal situation would be incomplete without addressing the third-rail of American politics: welfare and other income-redistribution programs. In the simplest of terms, these programs—sometimes called "entitlements"—are those federal expenditures that are guaranteed by law to some class of individuals. Traditionally, this refers to those programs like Social Security through which taxpayers pay into trust funds that are then distributed to the covered class with the expectation that they will receive benefits in kind when they become eligible. Because these payments are mandated by federal law, the programs effectively operate on autopilot. We hate that some call these programs "uncontrollable." They are certainly controllable, it is just that Congress refuses to control them.

When considering the fact that most income-transfer programs didn't exist a century ago, it is astonishing that they have grown to encompass so much of the federal budget. In 2019, mandatory expenditures like entitlements made up more than 62 percent of the total budget.

The rapid pace at which entitlements have consumed the federal budget is most visible when we examine the amount of public income-transfer payments each year, shown in Figure 3-8. An income-transfer payment is a redistribution of wealth from one individual to another without compensation. In 1980, the federal government only redistributed about $200 billion. By 2020, the amount of income-transfer payments had grown by twelve times to nearly $2.5 trillion.

It is ironic that when LBJ created the modern-day welfare state, he stated that the "days of the dole are numbered in America." Well, we are well beyond day 15,000, and the welfare state is larger and has captured more Americans into its grasp than ever before.

Figure 3-9

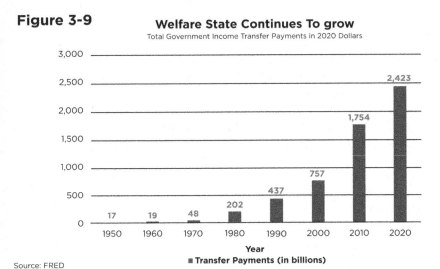

Source: FRED

Red Ink Rising

Perhaps the most concerning aspect of our current fiscal situation is the amount of taxpayer dollars being spent to service our mounting debt. As our national debt has grown year upon year, so, too, has the amount we spend every year on interest payments. All told, net federal interest expenditures consumed around 8 percent of the total federal budget in 2019. Figure 3-10 shows the increase in net federal interest expenditures.

- In 1940, the net interest on the national debt was less than $1 billion

- By 1980, the net interest on the national debt had grown modestly to around $52 billion

- In 2020, the federal government reported spending over $376 billion on financing the interest on our national debt

- Net federal interest expenditures in 2020 are approximately 418 times larger than they were in 1940

- Net federal interest expenditures have grown well over 40,000 percent between 1940 and 2020

Figure 3-10

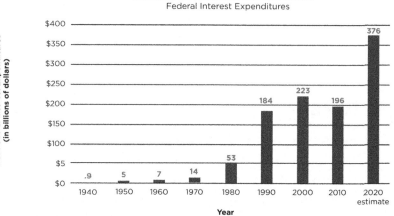

Growth of Interest on the Debt
Federal Interest Expenditures

Source: WH Historical Tables

As high as these numbers are, they are still misleading. Low interest rates in recent years mean that net interest expenditures are artificially low and, therefore, will increase even further as rates begin to rise.

It is also important to keep in mind that the 8 percent of the budget that goes to interest payments does little if anything to pay down the principal of our national debt. Instead, that $376 billion is effectively wasted taxpayer dollars. It is money that, if the government was fiscally responsible and not in debt, would not be spent at all and left rightfully in the wallets of taxpayers. Instead, it goes straight into the creditors' pockets as pure profit.

With foreign governments purchasing more of our debt each year, a significant portion of these interest payments goes directly to countries like China, Japan, and the United Kingdom, which collectively hold more than $2.7 trillion of our debt. When taken together, foreign countries and individuals hold more than $7 trillion, or about one-quarter of the current national debt.

Of course, this trend is a direct result of Congress' decision to continually spend with reckless abandon. The rise of our national debt necessitates appropriating ever-increasing sums to finance the interest on our debt. As shown in Figure 3-10, the growth in net interest payments is a direct consequence of the ballooning national debt.

- In 1950, each American family's share of the national debt was around $6,500
- By 2000, the share of the national debt per family had risen to nearly $49,000
- 2020 saw each family's share of the national debt grow to over $322,000
- Each family's share of the national debt has increased by nearly fifty times in the last seventy years.

Figure 3-11

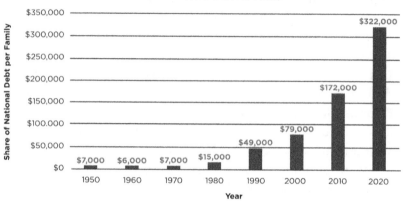

Americans' Second Mortgage
Federal Debt Per Family

Source: WH Historical Tables | Census Bureau

States Join the Spending Surge

Reckless spending is not just a federal phenomenon. In recent decades, states have also increasingly been mortgaging their financial future for the sake of perceived short-term gains. Although balanced-budget requirements and other fiscal restraints mean that states and localities cannot finance wasteful spending in the same way as the federal government, states are spending more taxpayer money than ever.

Figures 3-12 shows how state spending per capita has climbed in lockstep with federal spending over the last few decades. Since 1960 state and local spending has risen fivefold.

Figure 3-12

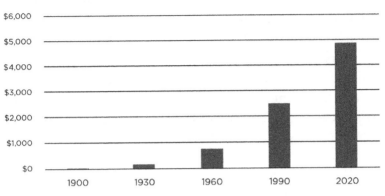

Per Capita State Government Spending (2012 dollars)

California is the textbook example of financial mismanagement. Prior to COVID-19, California faced a $54 billion budget deficit and a $580 billion debt. The American Legislative Exchange Council's annual report, *Rich States, Poor States*, ranked California number 45 in overall economic outlook. Similarly, Truth in Accounting rated California with an F for fiscal health and budget management in their annual *Financial State of the States* report, ranking them number 43 overall. In spite of this, California continues to spend lavishly on social programs and direct payments to individuals.

California is not alone. Across the nation, blue states in particular have been increasingly spendthrift. Some of this is due to their own poor financial decisions, but a significant portion comes from federal mandates. In a sort of *reverse-federalism*, the federal government has consistently imposed new burdensome mandates on states, relying on the states themselves to fund compliance.

In this sense, the federal government continues to pass the buck for mostly unfunded mandates like No Child Left Behind or the Clean Air Act.

Of course, the explosion of state budgets is not totally caused by federal mandates. Many states have spent extravagantly on superfluities. Citizens Against Government Waste, renowned for its annual "Pig Book" that compiles the worst-of-the-worst of federal pork-barrel spending, has released several reports outlining state-level pork. Below follow some of the most egregious cases from the past two decades:

- In 2011, Tennessee paid a whopping $140 million for a German company to relocate to Memphis

- In 2009, while facing layoffs due to a $1.8 billion budget deficit, Louisiana paid out nearly $30 million in overtime to the Department of Health and Hospitals and the Louisiana State Police Department

- In 2008, California spent over $1 million to buy fifty-one vans for the California Highway Patrol that "sat almost entirely idle"

- In 2006, Pennsylvania gave PNC Bank—a firm with assets totaling over $100 billion in 2006 and nearly $475 billion in 2021—$30 million to build a new office, condominium, and retail location

Spending at City Hall

Unfortunately, the trends at the federal and state level are also seen in counties and localities across the country. Similar to the previous chart, Figure 3-12 shows the growth in local government spending per capita over the past century. Since 1960, local spending has increased fourfold.

Clearly, the federal government's poor spending habits

Figure 3-13

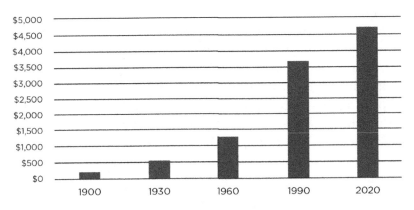

Per Capita Local Spending (2012 dollars)

have trickled down to the state and local level. In fact, the state and local situation has gotten to the point where the federal government has stepped in. Ostensibly because of the economic impact of COVID-19, the 117th Congress narrowly approved $350 billion in bailouts for states, counties, municipalities, and tribal governments as part of the American Rescue Plan Act.

It's unfortunate that Congress failed to learn from the mistakes of the Bank Bailout of 2008. Injecting federal funds into failing institutions merely delays the inevitable at the expense of the American taxpayer.

The Most Government Money Can Buy

In order to get a comprehensive snapshot of the fiscal health of our nation across the decades, we can combine the data from all three levels: federal, state, and local. When doing so, the unsustainability of this trend becomes even more apparent.

In the early 1900s, government in America was still relatively lean and constrained. At the turn of the 20th century, total government expenditures were around less than $10 billion. Now, total government spending tops $7 trillion, in just over a century. This trend shows definitively that government really has been America's fastest-growing industry.

Sums in the magnitude of trillions can be incredibly difficult to comprehend when the median family only makes around $69,000 per year. One of the best ways to put this situation into perspective is by examining government spending as a percentage of our economic output. Comparing the growth in government spending to the Gross Domestic Product (GDP) in Figure 3-14 clearly demonstrates how government has grown faster than the American economy.

Figure 3-14

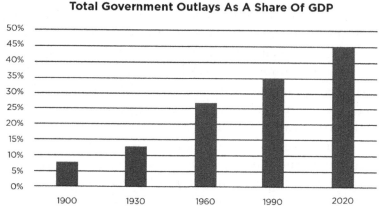

Total Government Outlays As A Share Of GDP

Source: usgovernmentspending.com

In 2020, thanks to trillions of COVID-19 relief funding, government was almost half of the U.S. GDP. This was supposed to be temporary, but Biden wants to make these programs permanent fixtures in the federal budget.

Total government spending has also outpaced population growth. As shown in Figure 3-15, government spending per household in 1940 was a mere $1,000. In 2020, that number has grown over seventy times to where the government spends an egregious $75,000 per household.

Figure 3-15

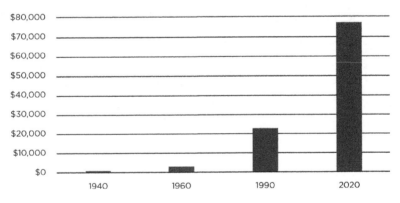

Total Government Spending Per Household

Sources: usgovernmentspending.com | Census Bureau

Very few American households believe that they receive $75,000 worth of public goods and services each year. Even fewer households could believe that they receive seventy-plus times as many services today as they did forty years ago. Yet, the gravy train continues to roll along.

A Gallup poll from 2014 confirms this sentiment. When asked "How many cents of each tax dollar would you say are wasted?" respondents said that 51 cents of every federal dollar are wasted. State and local governments received kinder treatment, with respondents saying 42 cents and 37 cents for every dollar are wasted, respectively.

Figure 3-16

Americans Believe Roughly Half Of Federal Spending Is Wasted

How many cents of each tax dollar would you say are wasted?

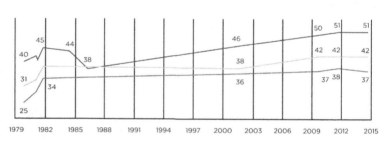

These results are far from an endorsement of government spending. To put this into perspective, Gallup's poll showed that Americans think that over $3.2 trillion of our $6 trillion budget for FY 2021 was wasted. Looking at the goods and services received by the public, it is difficult to argue with this opinion.

Conclusion

Benjamin Franklin's *The Way to Wealth* contains numerous aphorisms, but none are quite as cogent as Franklin's opinions on debt, for "as *Poor Richard* says, the second vice is lying, the first is running in debt."

For half a century, our government has continued to mortgage America's future. The fact that the United States credit rating on the Standard & Poor's in 2011 was downgraded is testament to this reality. As government spending has grown, so, too, has government borrowing, digging our hole deeper and deeper.

Sooner or later, our lack of common-sense fiscal restraint will catch up to us. At that point, even radical spending cuts may not be enough to save us. It is far better for politicians and pundits to make the tough decisions now than to wait until we tumble headlong off the looming fiscal cliff.

In Franklin's words, "If you would know the value of money, go and try to borrow some; for, he that goes a borrowing goes a sorrowing." Unless we act now, America will soon be sorrowing.

Chapter 4
THE TAX MAN COMETH

*When men get in the habit of helping them-
selves to the property of others, they cannot be
easily cured of it.*

—*New York Times* editorial slamming the
proposed Constitutional amendment legiti-
mizing the income tax in 1909

This book not only documents the awesome growth of
government in America over the last one hundred years,
but it also chronicles why we have allowed it to happen.
What were the seminal events that opened the Pandora's
Box of runaway government spending and intrusions into
our lives?

One clear factor was arguably one of the nation's
greatest mistakes: the introduction of a federal
income tax, which was a product of America's original
"progressive movement." Prior to 1900, a natural restraint

on government was that the taxing power was highly constrained by the Constitution. And since we lived under a moral code––long abandoned––that massive debt spending was only justified during times of national emergency, tax revenues became a de facto cap on government spending.

Throughout most of our first 125 years as a nation, most government receipts arrived via two forms of collections: land sales and revenue tariffs imposed on imported goods and products. Direct federal taxation of the citizens was prohibited constitutionally. Throughout most of the first century of our nation, the advocates of big government (what we would call today as "progressives") were frustrated in their attempts to expand government programs. There simply wasn't enough money in the federal fisc to pay for the ambitious dreams of the progressives of yesteryear.

This was why the movement to create a federal income tax was so fervently supported by the big-government advocates. The Progressive Era of a century ago could not have been made possible without this massive fountain of new revenues into the Treasury.

The 16th Amendment authorized for the first time the collection of a national income tax. But it was sold under false pretenses. The idea was that the income tax rate would never go above 7 percent. It would be a very low flat rate tax on incomes above a certain threshold, which spared the poor and many in the middle class from paying much, if any, income tax from their paychecks. In fact, when the first income tax was debated in Congress, an amendment was brought to constitutionally cap the tax at a rate of 10 percent. The advocates of the income tax voted that provision down by arguing that such a cap would really become a floor, and that no reasonable man believed the income tax would rise to the towering level of 10 percent. The cap was scuttled and, by the way, once America was dragged into World War I, the income tax soared to the once-unimaginable rate of 70 percent. In five years the rate skyrocketed from 7 percent to 70 percent.

The first income tax had monumental opposition among the citizenry. Even back in 1913 when it was passed, the 16th Amendment was incredibly controversial. Most constitutionalists, who were devoted to the founding idea of limited government, recognized the boundless potential for evil that the income tax presented. In fact a book was written in this era called: *The Income Tax: The Root of All Evil.*

Even the *Washington Post* and the *New York Times* were critical of the tax (these were different times than today).

Here are what a few of the critics said:

> "A vicious, inequitable, unpopular, impolitic, and socialistic act," complained *The New York Times* of the first income tax to pass Congress in 1894. It went on to say that the tax was "the most unreasoning and un-American movement in the politics of the last quarter-century."

> "It is an abhorrent and calamitous monstrosity," wrote *The Washington Post* of the idea of a graduated income tax in that same year. "It punished everyone who rises above the rank of mediocrity. The fewer additional yokes put around the necks of the people, the better."

The income tax was eventually ratified because its supporters promoted it as a levy that would fall only on the wealthiest Americans while exempting the middle class from the pain. Rep. Cordell Hull, who drafted the first income tax, argued that its purpose was to force "the Carnegies, the Vanderbilts, the Morgans, and the Rockefellers with their aggregated billions of hoarded wealth" to pay a fair share of the tax burden.

If this sounds familiar, it is because modern-day progressives are consistently using these very same arguments as Rep. Hull to justify their foolish attempt to "soak the rich" with new taxes. If you were to swap out the names in Hull's remark for Bezos, Musk, Zuckerberg, and Gates, the result is almost prophetic.

Congress has consistently used the progressive call to "soak the rich" as a ruse to get the proverbial camel's nose under the tent so that they can eventually raise taxes on the middle class. As we have seen time and time again, hikes in the top marginal tax rates never result in the revenue increases that progressives expect to see. As a result, rates on the lower tax brackets are raised in order to make up the difference.

Since the aftermath of World War I, which saw the first broad-based income levy, the income tax has been recognized by politicians as the single most powerful cash generator in the federal government's arsenal.

The secret of the income tax, however, is that it has never been a "rich man's tax" that "soaks the rich." Even when top rates hit their high around the end of World War II, Congress has gathered added revenues from the income tax only by imposing a larger share onto the backs of the middle class. This has been achieved by gradually increasing the number of taxpayers required to file returns and by raising not so much the marginal tax rates on the rich but the average effective tax rates on the middle class.

The bottom line is this: once the tax was instituted, any revenue constraints on government were toppled. And though the 70 percent tax rate implemented under one of the most liberal presidents in American history, Woodrow Wilson, fell back to 25 percent after the Harding-Coolidge tax cuts in 1923, the dam was broken forever. The rates during the FDR presidency rose to as high as 77 percent and then even to 90 percent. The *New York Times* was right: once government felt comfortable snatching money out of worker's paychecks, it became a habit—a habit that endures to this day.

When we look at the history of our country, it is always critical to remember why we fought for our independence. Being governed by leaders far removed from and not responsive to them, Patriots decided that taxes had become oppressive and unfair. This was the essence of the first major political rebellion on these shores—an event we all remember as the Boston Tea Party. This uprising and cries of "no taxation without representation" by the colonists was a springboard for the American Revolution. And the rest is history.

As a footnote, King George III allegedly declared when the British agreed to American independence, "the Americans have won their crusade of 'no taxation without representation.' Let's see how they like taxation with representation." He was right. The tax man's presence in our lives today would have been unimaginable during the founding of our nation. Much of the discontent among the Patriots related directly to one thing: taxes.

As our government has grown more and more tax hungry with every passing year, it is history worth recalling.

Taxes Take More than One-Third of Everything You Earn

If somebody asked the average American how much they pay in taxes annually, most would not be able to say, though they would surely answer that they pay too much. Given how complex the tax code itself is, not to mention the indirect taxes paid in the form of higher prices of goods and services resulting from taxes ostensibly on businesses but inevitably passed along to consumers, this is no surprise.

As seen in Figure 4-1, Americans work more than one-quarter of the year just to pay taxes. This doesn't include hidden taxes that families pay in the form of reduced wages via employee and employer share of Social Security, gasoline, and other excise taxes, state and local sales taxes, passed on corporate income taxes, taxes on production of goods and services, and other forms of taxation.

Figure 4-1

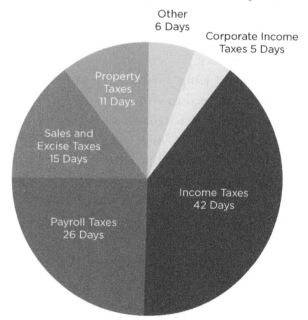

Americans Worked 105 Days of the Year to Pay Taxes

Other 6 Days

Corporate Income Taxes 5 Days

Property Taxes 11 Days

Sales and Excise Taxes 15 Days

Income Taxes 42 Days

Payroll Taxes 26 Days

Source: Tax Foundation

Needless to say, there are numerous forms of taxation that the government imposes on American families that go far beyond what the eye can see on a tax form or a pay stub. While a minimum of government is necessary, above a certain amount of spending—10 to 20 percent of what is produced each year, every dollar above that amount taken out of the private sector and given to the government is a dollar less efficiently used. It is also representative of increased costs to consumers, no matter the good or service.

Under the tax plans presented by President Biden in his "American Jobs Plan"—including increasing the corporate tax rate to 28 percent, the top individual income tax rate to 39.6 percent, and nearly doubling the capital gains tax rate from 23.8 percent to 43.4 percent, among other increases—there is no doubt families will pay more. Even without these increases in place, they already are.

According to the Tax Foundation, the average state and local tax burden per capita in 2018 was $5,755. At the federal level, Americans paid a whopping $1.53 trillion in income taxes alone in 2018.

The Tax Bite Over Time

All of these facts and figures demonstrate the simple point that, when combining federal, state, and local taxes, many middle-class Americans' income goes more to Uncle Sam than it does to themselves or their families. But this wasn't always the case. As Figure 4-2 shows, the percentage of national income taken up by taxes has grown significantly since the turn of the 20th century.

- In 1900, total taxes only accounted for 7.8 percent of the Gross Domestic Product (GDP), with federal taxes taking up 3.22 percent

- By 1930, taxes took up 14.6 percent of national income, with federal taxes sitting at 5.2 percent

- In 1960, total taxes took up 26.9 percent of GDP

- Between 1930 and 1960, state and local taxes remained relatively low, while federal taxes grew to account for 17 percent of GDP

- By 1990, total taxes had grown to 32.3 percent of GDP, with the federal share rising slightly to 17.3 percent

- Total taxes rose slightly from 1990 to 2020 to reach 33.2 percent of GDP

- In 2020, state and local taxes make up a larger share of GDP as the Tax Cuts and Jobs Act decreased federal taxes to 16.3 percent of GDP

Figure 4-2

Federal, State and Local Taxes as a Share of GDP

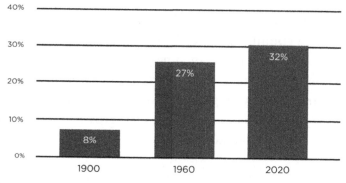

Source: US Government Historical Tables

According to the Tax Policy Center, "federal, state, and local government receipts totaled $5.4 trillion in 2018," and "federal receipts were 64 percent of the total." As previously stated, it is hard to put $5 trillion into perspective, so a better way to demonstrate the total tax burden is on a per-household basis, as shown in Figure 4-3.

Figure 4-3

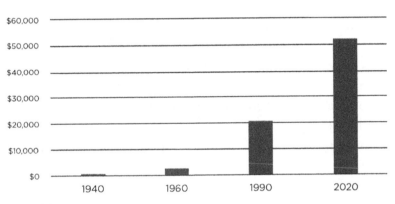

Total Government Taxes Per Household

Source: Tax Foundation

Taxes have gone from about $2,000 in 1960 to over $50,000 today.

Taxes are now one of the largest expenditures in the family budget. Based on the Bureau of Labor Statistics' Consumer Expenditure Survey, Americans spend more on taxes than they do on food, utilities, healthcare, debt payments, or savings. Americans only spend a larger share of their income on two categories: housing and transportation. Because these are aggregated statistics, it is likely that many Americans spend more on taxes than any other expense given the complexity of the tax system.

How Washington Raids Our Paychecks

There is an old saying in Washington about taxes. The goal of the politicians is to extract the most amount of feathers from the goose with the least amount of squawks.

In his first inaugural address in 1801, Thomas Jefferson urged his fellow citizens that "a wise and frugal Government, which shall restrain men from injuring one another, shall leave them otherwise free to regulate their own pursuits of industry and improvement, and shall not take from the mouth of labor the bread it has earned. This is the sum of good government...."

Just over the first one hundred years of our nation's history, the founders' philosophy of limited government, and limited taxation by extension, mostly prevailed. In 1800, the federal government only took an average of about $43 from each citizen in today's dollars. By 1900, that amount had risen modestly to $239 per citizen. Around the post-World War II period is when the explosion in taxation began.

In 1940, the average citizen was being taxed to the tune of $755, and by 1980 each citizen's share of federal tax revenues was $6,400. Today, federal taxes per capita top $10,000.

The Income Tax Monstrosity

Let's return for a minute to that seminal event we mentioned above, passage of the 16th Amendment, which formally authorized an income tax. What no one expected at the time was how high the tax rates would go:

- Implemented at 7 percent in 1913, it only took proponents of the income tax three years to break their promise with the highest marginal rate being raised to 15 percent in 1916

- The next year (1917), the highest marginal tax rate skyrocketed to 67 percent as America found itself embroiled in World War I

- World War II saw the second major spike in taxes with the top marginal tax rate peaking at an incomprehensible 94 percent in 1944 and 1945

- Top marginal tax rates didn't recede until the latter half of the Cold War, set at 72 percent in 1970, and hitting near record low of 28 percent in 1989 as the Berlin Wall fell

- Since the turn of the 21st century, the top marginal tax rate has hovered between 35 and 40 percent

What is fascinating, however, is that even when rates hit 70, 80, or even 90 percent, the share of GDP collected by the income tax has been remarkably constant. Higher tax rates do a lot of damage to the economy, but they don't raise much revenue because the super-rich like Bill Gates, Jeff Bezos, and Warren Buffett find loopholes, lawyers, and lobbyists to get around paying.

The Biden Tax Hike

Now let's look at what happens to tax rates under the Biden Tax Plan. In short, tax rates go up across the board.

Figure 4-4

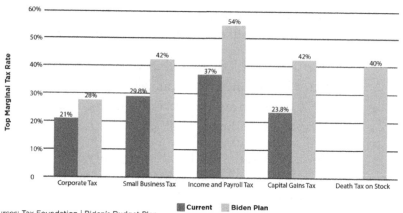

Biden's Progressive Top Marginal Tax Rates

Sources: Tax Foundation | Biden's Budget Plan

If Senate Budget Chair Sanders' dreams come true, the top marginal tax rate would again rise to 52 percent, while President Biden's plan calls for a rather arbitrary 39.6 percent coupled with corporate tax rate hikes. But when the 12.3 percent payroll tax he wants to apply to incomes above $400,000 is added to the equation, the effective tax rate climbs to 52 percent.

Biden would raise these tax rates to higher than rates in many other nations, including China. He believes that this is the way to make "the rich pay their fair share. But the chart below shows that lower tax rates have tended to correspond to higher tax collections because at high tax rates, economic activity is reduced and tax avoidance rises, as shown in Figure 4-5. The chart also shows that today the top 1 percent of earners pay more than 40 percent of all income taxes. So much for the rich not paying their fair share of taxes.

Figure 4-5

Lower Tax Rates, Higher Revenues

Low Rates = More Revenue

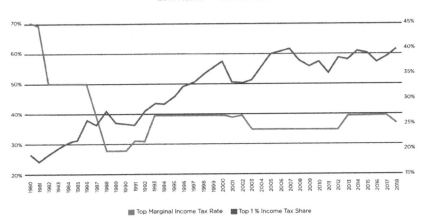

Top Marginal Income Tax Rate Top 1 % Income Tax Share

There can be no question that the income tax has served as one of the most powerful engines of governmental growth in this century. To understand this, we need only look at federal receipts from the income tax. In 1945, when the top marginal tax rate hit its peak, individual income taxes raised only $18.3 billion. In 2018, the Tax Foundation estimates that individual income taxes raised nearly $2 trillion of the $4 trillion in total revenue.

Federal tax receipts from individual income taxes have continued to rise even as the top marginal rate dropped and then plateaued. The only explanation for this trend is that the middle-class has consistently been paying more in income taxes.

Convoluted and Complicated Compliance Costs

One way to measure the increased complexity of the income tax code since its inception is to examine the mountain of forms and paperwork that it now requires. The original 1040 form was a total of four pages long— including the instructions that the *New York Times* published in its entirety on a single newspaper page. Now, while the 1040 form itself is still relatively simple, there is an added mountain of paperwork required for the average person to tell the federal government how much they owe.

Considering the total number of pages in the federal tax code paints a darker picture. (See Figure 4-6)

- In 1913, there were only 400 pages of federal tax law

- By 1960, there were 16,500 pages to the tax code

- Now, there are well over 75,000 pages

Most distressing about this trend is that the Tax Reform Act, passed in 1986, was intended to "simplify" the tax code. Clearly, the Internal Revenue Service doesn't care much for Congressional restrictions.

Figure 4-6

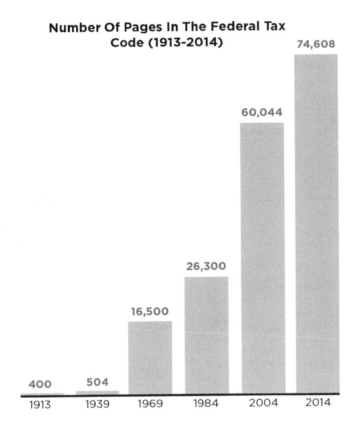

Number Of Pages In The Federal Tax Code (1913-2014)

Source: Washington Examiner

According to the National Taxpayers Union (NTU), Americans spent a combined eight billion man hours attempting to comply with the tax code in 2018. The implementation of the Tax Cuts and Jobs Act brought down that number to six billion hours in 2020, but NTU estimates that the net economic burden from tax compliance was still well over $300 billion. All this complexity is music to the ears of attorneys and tax accountants; it is maddening for the rest of us.

Another way to look at the complexity of the tax system is to examine the number of agents at the IRS, as shown in Figure 4-7.

Figure 4-7

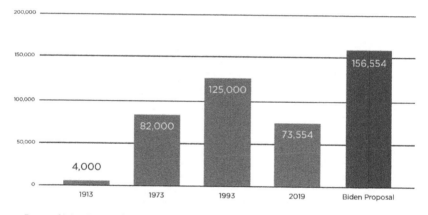

Growth In The Number Of IRS Agents

Source: Bureau of Labor Statistics | Biden Budget

To make matters worse, President Biden has called for doubling the IRS staff by adding another 87,000 agents.

Taxing Families First

Thanks, in no small part, to the rising tide of taxes, raising a family in the United States in 2020 is becoming untenable. The younger generations of Americans cite financial concerns as a primary reason they are choosing not to have children. According to a recent poll by Morning Consult, "3 in 5 childless millennials say a reason they don't have kids is because it is too expensive." While some of this can be attributed to the rising cost of housing and the student debt crisis, rising tax rates also have a major impact. Higher tax rates take away money that otherwise would be used to pay off student loans or purchase property.

High Taxes Stymie Economic Growth

Often wholly undiscussed is the massive indirect cost of government taxation on the economic activity in our country. Our governments at all levels discourage work and employment, personal savings and investment, and, perhaps most importantly, entrepreneurial investment that allows all of the preceding elements of our economy. There are no jobs without investment first.

Higher marginal tax rates on labor and capital than are necessary to fund the government also harm our economy to the tune of $300 billion in lost productivity every year. The inefficiency of the tax system is the primary driver of this loss. That is, if we had a simpler, flatter tax rate, the job-destroying and burdensome effects of taxes would be far lower than they currently are.

The State and Local Tax Burden

The tax burden imposed on Americans at the state and local levels has grown in concert with the federal tax burden. In 2019, the average state and local tax burden across the United States took up 10.3 percent of state income.

States also have followed Uncle Sam's lead by consistently becoming more dependent on income taxes as a source of revenues. Prior to World War II, only a handful of states imposed any sort of income tax.

Today, practically all states have some form of income tax, with far more states preferring a graduated tax to a flat income tax. The only places that do not have any form of statewide income taxation are Alaska, Florida, Nevada, South Dakota, Tennessee, Texas, Washington, and Wyoming.

According to the Census Bureau's accounting, in 2018, state and local governments raised a mind-boggling $487 billion in individual and corporate income taxes; one-third of the total state and local revenues of $1.49 trillion. Figure 4-10 outlines this trend by showing the rising share of income taxes as a percentage of total state and local taxes.

- In 1900, state and local governments raised none of their revenues from income taxes

- In 1960, state and local governments raised 10 percent of the revenues from income taxes

- In 2018, state and local governments raised 27 percent of their revenues from income taxes

That trend should be reversed. The nine states that do not levy an income tax have had about double the job creation of states like California, New Jersey, and New York with income taxes as high as 10 percent or more.

The lack of state income taxes is one huge reason that tech companies are fleeing incredibly highly taxed areas like Silicon Valley in California for greener pastures in Austin and Seattle. The people have been voting with their feet in favor of low income taxes.

Lower Tax Rates Can Mean More Revenues By Growing the Economy

Many might wonder, since Congress passed the Tax Cuts and Jobs Act in 2017 after the Bush tax cuts and the Reagan tax cuts prior to that, why are taxes still so high? This is certainly valid; however, tax hikes pass Congress far less noisily than tax cuts, and since the Reagan administration, many have made their way through.

Since the Reagan tax cuts in 1981, there have been tax increases in 1982, 1983, 1984, 1986, 1987, 1990, and 1993. These hikes essentially canceled many of Reagan's tax cuts—though the tax income tax rates wisely stayed low until George H.W. Bush broke his "READ MY LIPS: no new taxes" promise.

In fact, the whole experience of the Reagan tax cuts has been so thoroughly misrepresented that the mythology of the era has supplanted reality. This kind of historical revisionism is lethal. As the saying goes: "those who fail to learn the lessons of history are doomed to repeat them." So let's learn the real fiscal lessons of the Reagan era and dispense with the fairy tale.

The Reagan tax cuts did not cause the budget deficits of the 1980s. This is the ultimate distortion. Here's why: From 1980 through 1990, federal tax receipts in 1995 dollars doubled from $517 billion to $1 trillion. This was a 7 percent annual growth rate in tax revenues, or almost twice the rate of inflation. The problem is that federal outlays grew even faster.

As David Rosenbaum reported in *The New York Times* in 1992: "One popular misconception is that the Republican tax cuts cause the crippling federal budget deficit now approaching $300 billion a year. The fact is, the large deficit resulted because the government vastly expanded what it spent each year...."

The other popular myth about the Reagan tax cuts is that they were a huge tax cut for the rich. The problem with this reasoning is that in the 1980s the rich paid more taxes in total dollars and a larger share of the total tax burden.

Today, Democrats and leftists continue to make the same flawed arguments about President Trump's Tax Cuts and Jobs Act (TCJA). As shown in Figure 4-8, the result of both the Reagan era and the Trump tax cuts was that the tax structure got more progressive, with the rich paying a larger share.

Figure 4-8

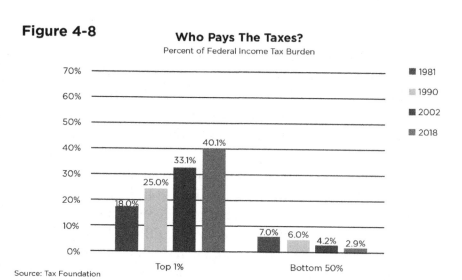

Who Pays The Taxes?
Percent of Federal Income Tax Burden

Source: Tax Foundation

Furthermore, despite the outcry from the left about budget deficits—which they seem not to care a whit about now that the spending spigot is turned on full blast—the

Trump tax cuts did not reduce federal revenues. TCJA did not hurt tax revenues. This was because tax cuts spur economic growth. In 2019 and 2020, tax revenues actually increased by $192 billion. The budget deficits we continue to see are instead caused by massive spending.

Washington has a spending problem, not a revenue problem. Tax cuts should be applauded.

Conclusion

In the famous Supreme Court case *McCulloch v. Maryland*, Chief Justice Marshall wrote: "The power to tax involves the power to destroy." Are we allowing taxes to destroy our country?

This question has been asked for decades now, and as long as taxes continue to hobble our economy, we will continue to agitate for a single flat-rate income tax. Or, better yet, a national sales tax that replaces the income tax entirely. We are paying a high price for the mistake of the progressive income tax enacted one hundred years ago and maybe it is time to correct it.

Chapter 5
THE REGULATORY OCTOPUS

It will be of little avail to the people, that the laws are made by men of their own choice, if the laws be so voluminous that they cannot be read, or so incoherent that they cannot be understood; if they be repealed or revised before they are promulgated, or undergo such incessant changes that no man, who knows what the law is today, can guess what it will be tomorrow. Law is defined to be a rule of action; but how can that be a rule, which is little known, and less fixed?

—Alexander Hamilton, The Federalist Papers #62

When Ronald Reagan ran for president in 1980, he promised to cut the "red tape" in Washington that was strangling our businesses. Then, thirty-six years later, Donald Trump won the presidency pledging to "drain the swamp" of Washington bureaucracy and rulemaking. Both temporarily succeeded in taking on the "deep state" in Washington, by which I mean the permanent governing class of lawyers, regulators, lobbyists, federal bureaucrats, and special interest groups that dominate the political process in America—and have done so for at least the last fifty years.

Alas, victories against the permanent ruling bureaucracy have been only temporary. In every instance, much like Darth Vader, the empire strikes back. In the first year of the Biden administration, the reregulation of America has been going on in full force.

Trump had made a commitment during the 2016 presidential campaign to "repeal two regulations for every new regulation." He actually dramatically under-promised and over-delivered. For every new regulation under Trump, not two, but eight existing rules were repealed. The White House estimated that the savings from deregulation under Trump were in the tens of billions of dollars.

But on the first day of his presidency, Joe Biden sat in the Oval Office and rescinded the Trump rule. He said he didn't want to "frustrate" the regulators and has given these unelected autocrats more power than ever. America is now under a new regime of regulatory assault, and it could shipwreck the economy if this new era of rulemaking is allowed to persist.

The Fourth Branch of Government

The United States Constitution lays out a relatively simple framework of three branches of government; but, in fact, we now have four. Federal regulatory agencies— for which there is no authoritative accountability—serve as a nonelected and extraconstitutional fourth branch. Of course, some regulations are important and have a positive impact on society. Some regulations, like requiring people to stop at stop signs, are common sense; others are well-intentioned but impose costs on our society that far outweigh any societal benefits. It is no accident that the super-regulator, Joe Biden, is trying to repeal cost-benefit-analysis rules, which are meant to ensure that our rulemaking is good for the country on-balance.

Although inexact, one method of measuring the size and scope of the federal regulatory burden is by examining the number of pages in the Federal Register. This daily publication by the Office of the Federal Register gives public notice of all proposed and finalized federal regulatory changes. Using the number of pages in the Federal Register as a proxy, Figure 5-1 shows how the number of federal regulations has grown significantly since the blossoming of the federal bureaucracy under Franklin Roosevelt in the 1930s. As we examine the ebb and flow of regulation over the past eighty years, we find that:

- In 1935, there were only 2,600 pages in the Federal Register

- By 1950, that number had grown to 9,600 pages

- In 1980, the number of pages in the Federal Register hit 73,000 under President Carter

- President Reagan's deregulatory agenda reduced the number of pages in the Federal Register to 50,000 in 1985

- In President Clinton's first full year in office, the number of pages in the Federal Register rose to 65,000

- This positive trend continued under Presidents Bush and Obama, with the number of pages in the Federal Register hitting 81,000 under President Obama in 2010

- During President Obama's last year in office, 2016, the number of pages in the Federal Register hit a peak of 96,000

- President Trump's deregulatory agenda initially slashed the number of pages in the Federal Register to 61,000 in 2016, with increases each following year

Figure 5-1

Number Of Pages In The Federal Register, 1936-2019

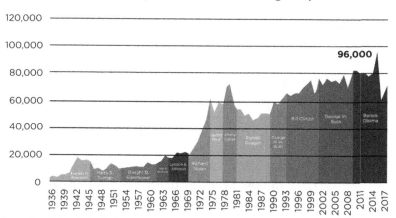

Source: Competitive Enterprise Institute

To put the size of the Federal Register into perspective, if you could stack a copy of each Register from the past two decades on top of one another, the tower would nearly reach the height of the Washington Monument; that's not including internal and external guidance documents and actions by independent agencies that are excluded from the Federal Register.

One other method of analyzing the growth of the administrative state is examining the number of "economically significant" final rules published in the Federal Register. The Office of Management and Budget (OMB) categorizes "major," "significant," and "economically significant" rules based on their "annual effect on the economy." Economically significant rules are those rules that are deemed to have an annual economic impact of $100 million or more "or adversely affect in a material way the economy…the environment, public health or safety, or state, local, or tribal governments or communities." In other words, economically significant rules are those regulations that have the largest negative impact on consumers and businesses.

Figure 5-2 demonstrates the general increase in the number of economically significant rules promulgated by each administration as compiled by the Regulatory Studies Center at George Washington University:

- There is nearly always a spike in the number of economically significant rules promulgated in each president's lame-duck year

- In 1981, President Reagan's administration implemented only a single economically significant final rule

- In 1990, George H.W. Bush's administration implemented thirty-four economically significant final rules

- President Clinton's lame-duck year in 1991 saw seventy-two economically significant final rules

- George W. Bush's lame-duck year in 2008 brought another seventy-three economically significant final rules

- President Trump's final year in office, 2020, saw the highest number of economically significant final rules with thirteen

Figure 5-2

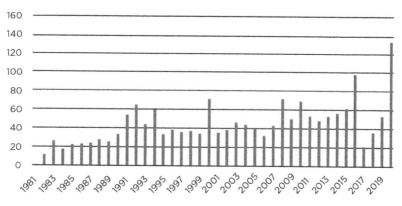

Economically Significant Final Rules Published Per Year, 1981-2020

Source: George Washington University

The growth in the size and scope of federal regulatory activities has necessitated steep growth in federal spending on these activities. In 1900, there were only ten regulatory agencies; today, by one account, there are 316. Figure

5-3 demonstrates this increased regulatory spending by showing the total amount of federal outlays for regulatory agencies as compiled by the Regulatory Studies Center at George Washington University:

- Over the last sixty years, federal outlays for regulatory agencies have increased by 1,625 percent

- In 1960, federal outlays for regulatory agencies amounted to about $4 billion

- By 2000, federal outlays for regulatory agencies had risen to nearly $34 billion

- In 2020, federal outlays for regulatory agencies were $65 billion, with $69 billion allocated for 2021

igure 5-3

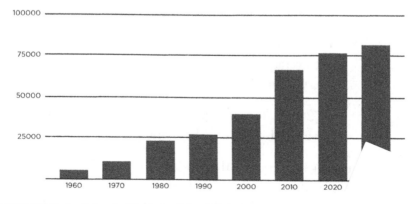

Federal Regulatory Agency Outlays, 1960-2021
(In Millions Of 2021 Dollars)

rce: George Washington University | Washington University in St. Louis

The Buck Doesn't Stop Here

This 30,000-foot view of the regulatory activity is an excellent indicator of the growth of the regulatory state, but the picture grows darker when considering the economic impact of this growth. According to the Competitive Enterprise Institute's annual report on regulation, *Ten Thousand Commandments*, the total annual cost for federal regulations alone is conservatively estimated to exceed $1.9 trillion based on publicly available data. That is excluding state and local regulatory burdens. The 2020 edition of *Ten Thousand Commandments* further explains these costs:

- The $1.9 trillion federal regulatory burden "is greater than the corporate and personal income taxes combined"

- On its own, the federal regulatory burden would be the eighth-largest economy in the world, right behind Italy

- The annual estimated federal regulatory burden per household is in the neighborhood of $14,500

- Per household, that "amounts to 18 percent of the average pretax household budget and exceeds every item in that budget, except housing"

- In 2019, "federal agencies issued 28 regulations for every bill passed" by Congress

Figure 5-4 is a graphical representation of the federal regulatory burden since the end of the Reagan Era. As you can see, the federal regulatory burden in the decades preceding the turn of the millennium averaged a not-insignificant $550 billion. By the second inauguration of President Obama, the federal regulatory burden jump 173 percent to approximately $1.8 trillion and has moderately increased every year hence.

Figure 5-4

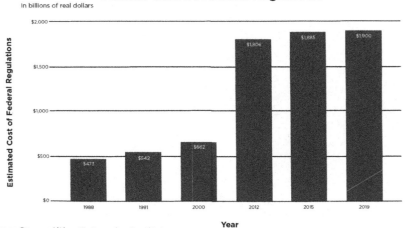

Annual Cost Of Federal Regulation

In billions of real dollars

Source: Competitive Enterprise Institute

The reprieve from massive regulatory costs has almost certainly come to an end with Joe Biden in the White House. Figure 5-5 shows that Biden has shot out of the gate signing new rules and imposing more red-tape requirements on business.

Figure 5-5

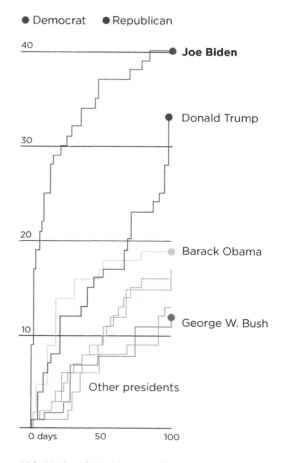

Cumulative Executive Orders In The First 100 Days Of Each Presidency

Data Collected From: U.S. National Archives and Records Administration

Source: The Wall Street Journal

Whereas Trump promised to repeal three regulations for every new regulatory edict, one of Biden's first executive orders was to repeal the Trump deregulation efforts. Biden is now busy rebuilding the super-regulatory state. In July of 2021 he signed an executive order that AP News described as: "Biden Signs Order Targeting Big Business." The new order places a new regulatory spotlight on big tech, Wall Street, healthcare, and the service sector of the economy. It deals with every industry from drug stores to airlines to hearing aids to internet services.

Chapter 6
WELCOME TO THE SWAMP

[King George III] has erected a multitude of New Offices, and sent hither swarms of Officers to harass our people, and eat out their substance.... We have appealed to their native justice and magnanimity, and we have conjured them by the ties of our common kindred to disavow these usurpations, which, would inevitably interrupt our connections and correspondence. They too have been deaf to the voice of justice and of consanguinity.

—The Declaration of Independence

Everything you need to know about Washington is summarized in one simple statistic: three of the five wealthiest counties in the United States are in or around the Washington D.C. beltway.

How did that happen? Washington doesn't produce anything except lawyers, lobbyists, regulators, politicians, government bureaucrats, and other do-gooders.

The old saying about our nation's capital is absolutely true: Washington is a place where people come to do good, and end up doing well. Many millions of people have gotten rich off the $50 trillion welfare state. Not many of them are poor people.

We have replaced what President Eisenhower rightly warned about—a "military industrial complex," with a "climate-change industrial complex." Regardless of what one thinks about global warming, and its impact on the future of the planet, what is absolutely certain is that many people are getting very rich off the hundreds of billions of dollars spent on climate-change programs in Washington and in the states.

Washington is a place filled with people who take; they don't make. They derive their power and prestige from usurping other people's incomes. Government at some level is necessary for our country to function. But it has reached a level of intrusiveness that is not additive, but subtractive to our national well-being. One theme of this book is that at nearly every level of government—but especially at the federal level—we could and should get better government results at half the price.

Ronald Reagan and Donald Trump are two recent presidents who came to take power away from the government and give it back to the people. Trump promised to "drain the swamp" and caused great indignation among the chattering class for starting to move agencies and functions of our federal government out of Washington D.C. But the elites in Washington have fought back. In Joe Biden they have elected a president who worships at the altar of big government. He has been told by his advisors that the bigger the government, the more successful the country will be. This is contrary to every instinct of our Founding Fathers and the American tradition for some 250 years.

What is unquestionable and troubling is that, right now, the swamp is winning.

The Bureaucracy: It Just Keeps Growing and Growing and Growing

According to the Bureau of Labor Statistics, as of May 2021, nearly 22 million Americans were employed by federal, state, and local governments. Local governments made up the majority of these jobs, accounting for 13.7 million government employees. The federal and state governments accounted for 2.8 and 5 million public sector jobs, respectively.

As large as these numbers are, they are likely underestimated. For example, the Office of Management and Budget's annual tally of federal full-time equivalent employment found that 4.3 million Americans worked for the federal government in 2020. Of those 4.3 million, 4.19 million—over 98 percent—were employed by the Executive Branch, with the remainder being split relatively evenly between the Legislative and Judicial Branches.

Employing 22 million Americans costs money, a lot of money. In fact, as Figure 6-1 demonstrates, state, and local government payroll on its own cost $140 billion in 2019. Figure 6-1 also shows the nominal increase in state and local payroll expenditures in the past few decades.

To my knowledge, the federal government keeps no authoritative accounting of their payroll. Fortunately, that is exactly what watchdog groups are for.

A 2017 report by Open the Books—whose stated mission is to "capture and post all disclosed spending at every level of government"—found that "the federal government disclosed 1.97 million employees at a cash compensation cost of $136.3 billion" for FY2016. As the report's topline makes clear:

- "The federal government pays its disclosed workforce $1 million per minute, $66 million per hour, and $524 million per day."

- "Over a six-year period (FY2010–2016), the number of federal employees making $200,000 or more has increased by 165 percent."

- "In FY2016, a total 406,960 employees made six-figure incomes—that's roughly one in five disclosed federal employees."

- "At 78 out of the 122 independent agencies and departments we studied, the average employee compensation exceeded $100,000 in FY2016." This compares with a median household income of closer to $68,000, and that is oftentimes with two parents working.

- "On average, federal employees are given 10 federal holidays, 13 sick days, and 20 vacation days per year. If each employee used 13 sick days and took 20 vacation days in addition to the 10 federal holidays, it would cost taxpayers an estimated $22.6 billion annually."

In spite of the fact that government employees rarely produce much economic value—and, more often than not, subtract economic value from the private sector—government employees are some of the best paid in the workforce. The trend of increasing expenditures on public payrolls is buoyed by the fact that government compensation is typically much higher than in the private sector. A recent report produced by the Heritage Foundation showed that, "according to the most recent data from the Bureau of Labor Statistics, average state and local employee compensation is 50 percent greater than private-sector compensation." Figure 6-1 shows the growth of state and local government employment.

Figure 6-1   **State And Local Government Monthly Payroll**

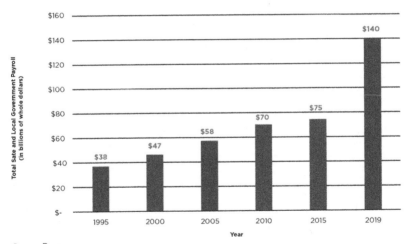

Source: Census Bureau

To put this into perspective, the number of Americans on government payrolls is approximately the same as the number of people living in the entire Northwest. Specifically, there are about the same number of people living in Idaho, Montana, Nevada, North Dakota, South

Dakota, Oregon, Utah, Washington, and Wyoming combined as there are working for the government.

Even adjusting for population growth, the number of individuals working for the government has grown throughout the decades. Figure 6-2 shows the growth in government employment as a share of the total civilian labor force.

Figure 6-2

Government Employees as a Percentage of Civilian Labor Force

Source: George Washington University | Washington University in St. Louis | Bureau of Labor Statistics

It is important to remember that a government worker can only have a job by taking income away from a private sector worker. Without the private sector workers and businesses, there would be no money for government to function or government employees to receive a paycheck. This is why "stimulating the economy" by spending more government money is a fool's errand. It is like taking a pail and collecting the water in the hull of a sinking ship and dumping the water into the other end of the ship.

All of this demonstrates the point that public sector employment has been one of America's fastest-growing industries. In fact, 1992 saw a turning point in this growth as government employment overtook manufacturing for the first time (see Figure 6-3). In short, the regulators have begun to outnumber the regulated. It used to be that we had three manufacturing workers for every government worker. Now we have more government workers than those who actually make things. That's depressing and dangerous.

Public Sector Workforce Now Greater Than Manufacturing Workforce

One amazing trend is the comparison between the manufacturing workforce and the government workforce. In earlier times in our history, manufacturing workers outnumbered government employees by a two-to-one ratio. Figure 6-3 shows that government employment now vastly exceeds manufacturing.

Figure 6-3

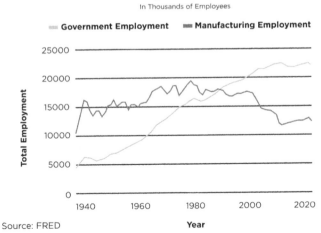

Government Employment Now Twice As High As Manufacturing
In Thousands of Employees

Source: FRED

Another trend worth noting has been the decline in private sector unionism versus the growth of public sector unions. Figure 6-4 shows the long-term decline in private unions. Meanwhile, government unions have doubled their membership. Today, for the first time ever, there are more public employees in unions than private sector workers in unions.

That is a big break from the past. For the first half of this nation's history, government unions didn't exist—or they were very rare. Even Franklin Roosevelt warned of the dangers of public sector unions because he recognized that if union officials were sitting across the table from the politicians (who collect campaign contributions from the unions), there would be no one representing the interests of the taxpayers. My, was he ever right. Since the dawning of the era of big government unions, the pay, the benefits, and the pensions have massively escalated.

Figure 6-4

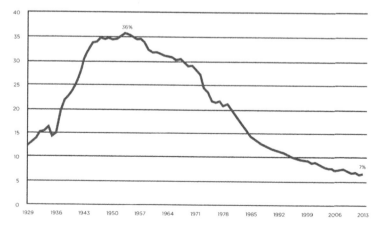

Percentage Of Private-Sector Workers Who Are Union Members

Source: Competitive Enterprise Institute

What is fascinating is that as private sector unionization continues to shrink to less than one of every eight private sector workers in a union today, public sector union membership is close to 50 percent.

The evolution of the American workforce over the past few decades has seen steadily shrinking union membership for practically every industry and occupation except one: government. Figure 6-4 contrasts the decline in private sector union membership to the growth of public sector union membership. Since 1985, private sector union membership has dropped by over 4 million. During the same period, public sector union membership has grown by nearly 1.5 million. In other words, the private sector has lost 36 percent of its union members while the union membership in the public sector has grown by nearly 20 percent.

As you can see, the public sector is consistently taking up more and more of total union membership.

- In 1985, public sector employees accounted for about one-third of total union membership

- In 2009, the public sector share of union membership crossed 50 percent for the first time

- Since 2009, this breakdown has remained relatively constant, with public sector employees making up about half of all union membership

The Federal Octopus

The average American doesn't see or even think about government employees unless they're registering their car at the DMV or being handed a traffic ticket. So, where are all of these 22 million public sector employees? An insightful and practically clairvoyant essay from 1930 entitled *Federal Octopus* is particularly cogent on this question. In describing the shocking similarities between the fertility of biological organisms and government agencies, the author wrote:

> "The bureau is, in the realm of government, what protozoa are in the realm of zoology. Originating as a single cell, they immediately begin to reproduce by fission, a self-division of the body into two or more complete cells, The protozoa abound in stagnant waters, as the bureau can flourish only in the stagnation of public spirit. Protozoa are parasites and the cause of certain diseases, as bureaus are parasitic and destructive of the vigor and health of the body politic. Again, protozoa are the simplest and lowest form of animal life, just as bureau government is one of the earliest and crudest form of arbitrary rule.
>
> Protozoa are apparently content to remain protozoa, but there the analogy ends; the bureau is ever striving onward and upward, and not only subdivides itself indefinitely, but each subdivision in turn seeks to elevate itself ultimately into a mighty department."

As Ronald Reagan put it, rule one of bureaucracy is protect the bureaucracy.

Reagan's aphorism is true as far as it goes, but Harry E. Teasley Jr. of the Mises Institute went one step further in outlining *The Seven Rules of Bureaucracy*:

Rule #1: Maintain the problem at all costs! The problem is the basis of power, perks, privileges, and security

Rule #2: Use crisis and perceived crisis to increase your power and control

Rule #3: If there are not enough crises, manufacture them, even from nature, where none exist

Rule #4: Control the flow and release of information while feigning openness

Rule #5: Maximize public-relations exposure by creating a cover story that appeals to the universal need to help people

Rule #6: Create vested support groups by distributing concentrated benefits and/or entitlements to these special interests, while distributing the costs broadly to one's political opponents

Rule #7: Demonize the truth tellers who have the temerity to say "the emperor has no clothes"

Due in no small part to these seven principles, the federal octopus has longer tentacles that touch more of American life than was ever thought possible. Throughout the country, federal administration buildings and courthouses stand as monolithic monuments to the almighty, omnipresent feds.

Figure 6-5 chronicles the growth of the federal bureaucracy over the past 230 years. The Founding Fathers saw fit to create just four cabinet agencies: The Department of State, The Department of War, the Department of the Navy, and the Treasury Department. Each of these had narrowly defined roles and were effectively powerless absent Congressional action. Now, there are sixteen cabinet-level departments, and, as discussed earlier, an uncountable number of lower-level agencies of varying degrees of independence.

Figure 6-5

Cabinet Level Department	Date of Founding
State	1789
Treasury	1789
Interior	1849
Agriculture*	1862
Justice**	1870
Commerce	1903
Labor	1913
Defense***	1947
Health and Human Services	1953
Small Business Administration	1953
Trade Representative	1963
Housing and Urban Development	1965
Transportation	1967
Environmental Protection Agency	1970
Office of Management and Budget	1970
Energy	1977
Education	1979
Veterans Affairs	1989
Homeland Security	2002

Source: White House

As astonishing as it may seem, for the first fifty years or so of our nation's history, effectively all domestic affairs were handled by a single agency: the Treasury Department. This is to say that the federal government did very little in the way of domestic policy, as the majority of these affairs were handled independently by the states. The Department of the Interior was created in 1849 with the stated mission of taking charge over the nation's domestic affairs.

Over the next hundred years, the federal octopus rapidly grew several new tentacles in the Departments of Agriculture, Justice, Commerce, and Labor. In the aftermath of World War II, bureaucratic growth went into overdrive, spawning ten new cabinet-level agencies between 1947 and 1979.

There have only been two cabinet-level Departments to end: the Department of the Navy (which was incorporated into the Department of Defense) and the Post Office, which was spun into an independent agency in 1970.

The Washington Edifice Complex

Beyond being the largest employer, the federal government is also the largest property owner. Just in terms of office space, the General Services Administration's Inventory of Owned and Leased Properties reports that the federal government owns and leases over "376.9 million square feet of space in 9,600 buildings in more than 2,200 communities nationwide." In terms of public lands, the federal government owns and manages approximately 28 percent of the entire landmass of the United States at around 640 million acres.

Taken together, these two facts mean that the federal government is one of—if not the—wealthiest landholder in the entire world. With these millions of acres being worth trillions of dollars, there is a good chance that selling off all of this land in one fell swoop could pay off our national debt.

Of course, this would be entirely impractical, especially given the sensitivity of our national parks, but it serves to show just how much of an impact the federal government has on our nation's economy.

Some states are harder hit than others by the consolidation of land in the hands of the feds. By the latest count in 2018:

- 80 percent of Nevada is administered by the federal government

- 63 percent of Utah is administered by the federal government

- 62 percent of Idaho is administered by the federal government

- 61 percent of Alaska is administered by the federal government

- 52 percent of Oregon is administered by the federal government

Awash in Lawyers

The growth of the federal government's control over the lives of everyday Americans has led to an explosion in the legal profession. As more Americans are finding it harder to navigate the litany of burdensome laws and regulations, more lawyers have been required to make sense of the oftentimes contradictory federal code. As Mark Twain reputedly put it, "the law is a system that protects everybody who can afford to hire a good lawyer."

Unfortunately, not everyone can afford to hire a good lawyer.

As James Davidson, former head of the National Taxpayers Union, documented in his book *The Great Reckoning*:

- In 1990, America had more lawyers than the rest of the industrialized world combined

- America has four times as many lawyers per person as Great Britain, five times as many as Germany, ten times as many as France, and almost twenty times more than Japan

- The lawyer surplus in America is so large that, in a typical year, more people graduate from law school at American universities than there are lawyers in Japan

Figure 6-6 demonstrates the growth in the world's second-oldest profession by showing the ratio of lawyers to the total U.S. population. Not shown in this chart is the fact that the legal profession rapidly began expanding following World War II, as more Americans and businesses were coming to grips with the expansion of the federal government during the era of the New Deal.

Figure 6-6

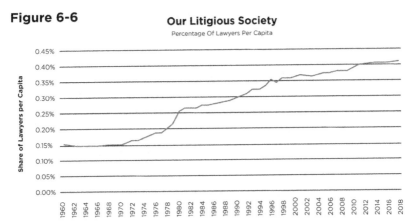

Our Litigious Society

Percentage Of Lawyers Per Capita

Sources: ABA and FRED

This trend is particularly prevalent in our nation's capital. In 2020, the D.C. Bar reported having 111,138 members with 65,690—59 percent—being primarily located in Washington. That means that approximately one-in-ten residents of the District of Columbia is a barred attorney. Clearly, the proliferation of the federal code has been particularly lucrative for attorneys.

The Litigation Explosion

There is an old saying that if you put one lawyer in a town, he goes bankrupt. If you put two lawyers in a town, they both get rich.

If you put thousands of lawyers in a town, they all get rich and everyone else loses.

Of course, lawyers do fulfill a very useful function in society. We are a nation of laws, and enforcing the rules of the game/economy are important to protect private property rights, to prevent crime, and to encourage risk-taking and enterprise—among other things.

But lawyers also use sharp elbows and political connections to ensure they are first in line in the rewards from big government. For example, class-action lawsuits often reward lawyers far more than victims of corporate wrongdoing. The big winners from tobacco settlements were lawyers and state governments—the people who got cancer, and the family members of those who died, got very little of the tens of billions of dollars of settlements. That was true also of financial fraud that occurred during the housing bubble. Lawyers cleaned up. In some cases with class-action suits, the lawyers get millions and the plaintiffs get hundreds.

Lawyers are also at the forefront of antitrust lawsuits against supposed "monopolies." Most economists agree that antirust is rarely the solution to market concentration. Lawyers are almost always first in line to promote antitrust regulations against American companies. Consumers never made money off of the Standard Oil, Microsoft, or AT&T antitrust suits. But the lawyers made bundles.

This should come as no surprise. After all, what do lawyers do best? Litigate. The year 2001 saw approximately 322,600 federal, civil, and criminal filings. By 2020, federal, civil, and criminal filings had jumped nearly one quarter to 425,945. Although it is tough to say with any certainty which way this causality runs, there can be no question that a good chunk of these lawsuits are frivolous and unproductive. To make matters worse, this excess of litigation creates a drag on our economy.

One report by the U.S. Chamber of Commerce examining just the U.S. tort system found that in 2016 the "total costs and compensation in the system amounted to $429 billion," only 57 percent of which went to plaintiff compensation. That means $184 billion of plaintiff compensation went directly into the attorney's pockets. The report further found that this "figure was equivalent to 2.3 percent of U.S. gross domestic product, or $3,329 per household in America."

The crisis of litigation in America is driving up the costs for everything from pharmaceuticals to automobiles. Take, for example, these stories of ridiculous lawsuits published by USA Today:

It started in 2013, when a teenager measured his Subway footlong sandwich. It turned out to be only 11 inches, an inch too short. Fast forward three years, and the company was settling a class-action lawsuit in court, promising to make its rolls 12 inches. The only people to benefit from the lawsuit were the *attorneys, who were about to receive $520,000 in fees. The judge agreed with activist and legal writer Theodore Frank that this was not fair and dismissed the settlement and the entire case.*

Red Bull's famous slogan "Red Bull gives you wings" got the company in some trouble. A class-action lawsuit accused the company of having misleading ads and making false claims. Plaintiffs said the energy drink did not give people wings, even figuratively speaking, that is, they didn't feel energized. They said the company lacked evidence to claim the beverage could improve one's focus. Red Bull settled out of court and agreed to pay $640,000.

A Tennessee man sued fast food chain Popeyes Louisiana Chicken for $5,000 for running out of its famous chicken sandwich because, he claimed, the restaurant wasted his time trying to fill his order. Craig Barr said the company deceptively advertised the sandwich, which was only available for a limited time in August. Barr is also suing for damages to his car that he said occurred at the restaurant's parking lot. The case was scheduled to go to court in January.

While each of these cases is its own particular brand of bizarre, it demonstrates how increasing litigation stifles economic growth. Harkening back to Bastiat's parable of the broken window, such ludicrous and frivolous lawsuits cost both time and money for both parties involved. Even for large corporations with strong legal departments, frivolous litigation is expensive and time-consuming, taking away resources from business growth and even legitimate litigation.

Excessive litigation imposes negative effects on the economy in many different ways, including:

- Diversion of business time and effort to fighting aggressive lawyers

- Overloaded court dockets that result in expensive delays

- Using "defensive medicine" to prevent against malpractice suits and other such cases

- A reluctance to innovate or bring new products to market for fear of litigation

The Influence Peddlers

The only group of people who seemingly outnumber lawyers in Washington, D.C., are lobbyists. To confuse matters more, there is a significant overlap since, oftentimes, attorneys are lobbyists and *vice versa*. The number of trade groups and associations in Washington has grown so rapidly that there is now an association for associations! Among other activities, The American Society of Association Executives engages in significant "advocacy and communications efforts [to] enhance recognition for the profession and result in a positive legislative and regulatory climate for the association community." In other words, they're lobbyists for the lobbyists.

- According to the ASAE, there were more than 92,000 professional and trade associations in 2010

- Established in 1958, the American Association of Retired Persons (AARP)—the largest association in America—has grown to be a Washington behemoth with an annual budget of over $850 million and 38 million members—about 12 percent of the total U.S. population

- According to OpenSecrets, there were 11,544 registered lobbyists in 2020, just at the federal level

- Total expenditures on lobbying in 2020 topped $3.5 billion

Super PAC Attack

Political Action Committees (PACs), and their younger brother Super PACs, are one of Washington's most ingenious inventions of recent times. Effectively created by the Supreme Court in the now-infamous case of *Citizens United v. FEC*, Super PACs are a special class of organization that is allowed to raise and spend unlimited amounts on political campaigns so long as they do not coordinate directly with the candidate.

Since the *Citizens United* decision in 2010, Super PACs have grown in size and number such that they now dwarf direct campaign spending. In the 2020 election cycle, there were 2,276 Super PACs, up from 83 a short decade ago. These Super PACs raised a total of $3.4 billion, and spent $2.1 billion. Figure 6-7 shows the growth in campaign contributions by Super PACs each election cycle.

Figure 6-7

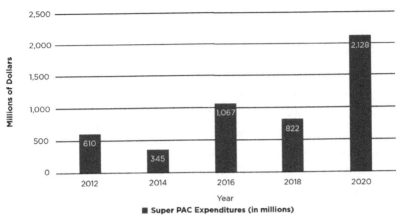

Campaign Contributions By Super PAC's

Sources: OpenSecrets

As you can see, campaign expenditures tend to decrease in nonpresidential cycles and skyrocket in presidential campaign years. Many Super PACs solicit donations to bolster their "war chest" during off years, allowing them to go full bore during election season. The result has been a massive political shift toward indirect expenditures.

Of course, Super PACs and other forms of independent campaign expenditure don't happen for no reason. While calling this system *quid pro quo* might be stretching the truth a bit, it's clear that, to paraphrase Dire Straits, politicians aren't getting money for nothing. In short, hiring lawyers and lobbyists, giving to Super PACs, and even direct campaign contributions are all ways that individuals, companies, and organizations seek to influence the levers of power in Washington.

There is nothing wrong with lobbying. Lobbying is a way to petition your government for grievances or to take action. It is as old as the Constitution. We submit that lobbying has grown at the pace of government spending and that is no coincidence. The more power we confer upon Congress to oversee the economy and to spend trillions of dollars, the more private parties will hire lobbyists as protection money to keep out of the crosshairs of the politicians, or to get a bigger slice of the pie in Washington.

I remember the days when very few Silicon Valley firms had lobbying offices in Washington. Their attitude was one of contempt of the political class and Washington. In the beginning of the tech boom, they believed in the doctrine: if we leave the politicians alone, they will leave us alone. How naïve. Even some of America's tech titans like Microsoft avoided for years a Washington presence. But then came the antitrust suits and other harassment by the politicians because Microsoft wasn't paying royalties to government. Today Microsoft, Facebook, Google, and Amazon have big Washington offices stacked with lobbyists. What a waste of resources. What a threat to American tech dominance. Do the politicians care?

Conclusion

Uncle Sam's multitude of "public servants" and other hangers-on are clearly "eating out the substance" of our productive private economy. What is troubling is the public's passive response to the rise of the bureaucracy and special interests. Government's take, whether in the form of bureaucratic compliance or influencing the process, is now accepted as an unavoidable cost of doing business. It is reminiscent of the days when mobsters and political machines ran our major cities in the 1920s and 1930s, demanding 10 percent off the top from businesses for "protection." The only difference is that the mob tended to let you run your business how you saw fit. And the mob only took 10 percent.

Today, corporate America, and small businesses too, write off this Washington "tax" as a "cost of doing business." But as we discovered in earlier chapters, that cost of doing business is escalating every year and the threat is going to get much worse in the future if Biden has his way.

Biden and the modern-day "progressives" don't seem to get what our American president one hundred years ago, Calvin Coolidge, well understood. Coolidge once captured the essence of politics when he observed in his autobiography that "nine-tenths of those who come to Washington want something they ought not to have." The primary reason that our government doesn't work anymore is that nine-tenths of the people who come to Washington now get what they ought not have.

Their gain has become America's loss.

Epilogue

TWENTY ONE STRATEGIES TO DEFEAT GOVZILLA

As we drift toward the fiscal abyss, I propose an interim measure: abolition of the words billion and trillion, words far too friendly to convey the enormity of the sums they are meant to denote. Politicians, in particular, should be forced to say thousand million for 'billion' and thousand thousand million for the flip 'trillion.'

It is a linguistic crime that the easy, two-syllable 'trillion,' hitched to a humble number like 4, should be permitted to express a debt that, had William the Conqueror begun saving for it in 1066 at the rate of $1 million a day, would still be unpaid today.

—Charles Krauthammer, *Washington Post*,
April 17, 1992.

Given the trends revealed in this book, it should be beyond any reasonable dispute that our nation is careening toward a financial cliff with catastrophic consequences for our economy—and our basic freedoms. Government is today truly and indisputably the fastest-growing industry in America. The enemy that threatens America is not a foreign adversary. It is from within—our own political class of elected leaders and the permanent governing ruling class in Washington—the Deep State—that has command and control of an ever-larger share of our nation's resources. By 2050, we could have a federal budget in which almost half of our spending is simply to pay the interest on the debt from previous years and decades.

These are the ramifications of what is happening right now in Washington. This isn't a threat that is ten, twenty, or thirty years ago. As the saying goes, the barbarians are truly at the gate, now. The Biden $6 trillion budget plan is a torpedo headed toward our ship of state. It will set in motion an endless cycle of 1) spend, 2) tax, 3) borrow, 4) print money, 5) inflate, and devalue the currency. Bankruptcy. Poverty. Despair.

So what are the steps that can and should be taken to avert this clear and present danger to the economic future of our nation? Here are twenty-one reforms that could restore freedom, prosperity, and balanced budgets:

1) FLAT TAX: Adopt a flat-rate income tax of 19 percent so that the U.S. tax code is simple, fair and understandable. If America has the lowest tax rates in the world, we win.

2) WORK FOR WELFARE: Require work as a condition of every government-assistance program. Welfare should be a hand up, not a

handout. Welfare reform in the 1990s under Bill Clinton and a Republican Congress was one of the most successful bipartisan programs in American history. Under Obama and now Biden, work-based welfare reforms have been eviscerated.

3) REPLACE GOVERNMENT GRANTS WITH LOANS: All government programs that give money to businesses, corporations, families, farmers, or unemployed individuals should be replaced by loans to be repaid to taxpayers by the recipients. Payments to businesses and families during a period of crisis, such as COVID-19, should be distributed in the form of low-interest loans to be paid back to the taxpayers over time. No free money.

4) NO FEDERAL DOLLARS TO MILLIONAIRES: Pass a law that disqualifies any company, corporation, or household with incomes or assets above $1 million from receiving government grants, loans, loan guarantees, or other forms of largesse. This should be called the Millionaire Exclusion Act. Sorry, Elon Musk—a billionaire who has received more than $5 billion of taxpayer assistance through all his ventures—no more government handouts.

5) TERM LIMITS ON CONGRESS: Limit terms of members of Congress to two six-year terms in the Senate and three two-year terms in the House. It will take a true citizen legislature to disrupt the evil "iron triangle" in Washington—lobbyists, career bureaucrats, and career politicians.

6) NO WELFARE FOR LOBBYISTS: Firms and other organizations should be permitted to take money from Washington or to lobby Washington—but not both. We cannot allow federal tax dollars to be used to subsidize the lobbyists. That is happening now with the myriad of liberal special interest groups that have been feeding off the Biden American Rescue Act money and are using those tax dollars to lobby for $6 trillion in more spending.

7) A FEDERAL SPENDING LIMIT: Institute an ironclad spending cap in Washington. Limit overall federal spending to the previous year's increase in population and inflation, with a two-thirds vote required in both houses of Congress. If spending exceeds that cap in any year, there should be an automatic across-the-board cut in every agency by an amount sufficient to bring spending down below the cap. Many states have added this requirement to their state constitutions, and it has put a leash on runaway government spending.

8) CREATE OPTIONAL PERSONAL SAVINGS ACCOUNTS AS AN ALTERNATIVE TO SOCIAL SECURITY TAXES: Give all workers in America the option of taking 10 percent of their paychecks and putting the money into an index fund of all American stocks. Instead of the money going into the government pension program, Social Security, workers would directly deposit the funds into their individual and worker-owned accounts until the age of sixty-five, or after. This would be optional and every worker would be given a monthly benefit guarantee no worse

than what Social Security would offer. Almost all workers would have an account after forty years of working that would pay out a monthly benefit between three and five times higher than Social Security offers. Also, any money not spent out of these accounts could be passed on to children tax-free at the time of death.

9) ALLOW THE PRESIDENT TO IMPOUND FUNDS: The president's historical power to impound funds—i.e., not spend money that has been appropriated by Congress—should be restored. It should take a vote of two-thirds of both Houses of Congress to override a presidential impoundment. A CEO has the authority to decide when money doesn't need to be spent. So should the president—or else we get massive wasteful spending on programs with no purpose or mission.

10) RAISE DOLLARS TO REDUCE THE NATIONAL DEBT BY ALLOWING DRILLING AND MINING ON FEDERAL LANDS: Allow environmentally friendly drilling and mining on federal lands to reduce foreign dependency, create hundreds of thousands of jobs, foster economic development, and raise money for the government. A study by the Committee to Unleash Prosperity finds that the U.S. is sitting atop a buried treasure of some $50 trillion of oil, gas, coal, minerals, and precious metals that are recoverable with existing technologies. The permitting rights and royalty payments alone would collect more than $10 trillion for Uncle Sam. Half of those revenues should be paid to the states where the mining and drilling

occurs. This would also reduce our trade deficit by trillions of dollars by producing energy here and not buying it from OPEC and other nations.

11) LET THE STATES BUILD THE INFRA-STRUCTURE: Devolve all federal infrastructure and transportation programs to the states. President Eisenhower's wise investment to link America through an interstate highway system was completed thirty years ago. We need to phase out federal involvement in local infrastructure projects by devolving programs and the 18.4-cent-a-gallon federal gas tax revenue to the states to set their own priorities, while encouraging innovation and private investment in toll roads and the like. One study by the Federal Highway Administration found that congestion pricing on highways would save $20 billion a year in transportation costs. Unfortunately, federal funding stifles these kinds of market-based reforms and inevitably diverts dollars to pork projects like train museums, turtle bypasses, and bridges to nowhere. Cliff Winston, a transportation economist at the Brookings Institution, estimates that "between 20 and 30 percent of federal transportation dollars" get eaten up in congressional regulations and mandates. The most costly of these by far is the Depression-era Davis Bacon Act, which virtually requires that on all federally funded projects inflated union wages get paid to the mostly all-union worker forces.

12) LET FEDERAL DOLLARS FOR EDUCATION GO TO PARENTS: Every dollar of federal education money should go to parents with kids

in school, not universities, school districts, and teachers unions. Parents in America should have public and private school options on where their kids go to school. Competition and consumer choice will save our schools. In most cities, a child can get a better education at roughly half the cost in the Catholic school system than in the public schools.

13) REQUIRE UNIVERSITIES AND COLLEGES TO FREEZE TUITION: Require that every college and university in America freeze its tuition costs for ten years as a condition of receiving any federal grants, aid, student loans, or other research grants. College tuition is bankrupting middle-class families and saddling our children with as much as $100,000 in debt. Tuitions have run at double the rate of overall inflation and increases in government loans and scholarships have only encouraged universities to raise their tuition.

14) END THE DEATH TAX: In a nation that believes in the free enterprise system, and honors the great American tradition of family-owned businesses, death should not be a taxable event. Parents should be able to pass on their businesses, ranches, farms and life-long savings to their kids and grandkids, rather than handing those assets over to the government. It is a quintessential American ideal that wealth is transferred as a legacy to the next generation, not to the politicians. Under the current laws, and those proposed by Biden, families will literally have to sell the farm to pay the death taxes. That's an outrage.

15) PRIVATIZE FEDERAL ASSETS: The Biden administration wants to give $65 billion to Amtrak. It is a railroad that has lost money every year for fifty years. Private operators could do a much more professional job. Let the private sector run the transit systems, the Postal Service, the schools, the airports and ports. These assets once transferred into private hands would provide more customer-friendly services at lower costs, and would pay taxes, rather than consume taxes.

16) MANDATE PASSAGE OF A CONSTITUTION TEST FOR HIGH SCHOOL SENIORS: States should follow Arizona's lead and require every high school student to pass a citizen's test on the Constitution, the Bill of Rights, and other seminal American documents. Passing this test should be a prerequisite before awarding a high school degree.

17) SHUTDOWN THE DEPARTMENT OF EDUCATION (DOE): Education is a state and community and parental responsibility, not that of the federal government. The terms "education" and "schools" do not even appear in the constitution. U.S. DOE spending over the past sixty years has been INVERSELY related to student performance.

18) REQUIRE CONGRESS TO VOTE ON ALL NEW REGULATIONS: Require Congress to vote to approve any rule or regulation promulgated by an independent agency, such as the SEC, FTC, FDA, and EPA, if that regulation has an economic impact above $100 million. Independent regulatory agencies are an unconstitutional delegation of lawmaking authority to unelected officials. Congress makes the laws, not presidential appointees.

19) ABOLISH ALL FOREIGN AID:—except for cases of economic or humanitarian emergency. Foreign aid programs have been a failure for decades, and private charity is far more effective than government to government handouts. The U.S. should withdraw from the IMF, OECD, World Bank, and other international organizations that do not put the interests of Americans first.

20) RETURN FEDERAL LANDS TO THE STATES: There should also be a policy of no net increase in federal land ownership. With the government owning almost half the land area west of the Mississippi, the government should be granting land to the states, or selling it to American developers. Any land purchases by the federal government should be offset acre for acre with an equal size sale of federal land. The states and private owners are far better custodians of our mountains, wilderness areas, deserts, and urban land than the government, as the forest fires out west attest to. In the first one hundred years of this nation, federal land sales were a major source of federal revenues, and they should be again.

21) NULLIFICATION POWER FOR STATES: Allow states to nullify federal laws if the nullification act is approved by two-thirds of the legislature and a vote of the people of the state. This will restore the rights of states to control their own destiny and provide the states and the people with protections against federal laws that discriminate against certain states.

Final Thoughts

It is a pretty good bet that our Founding Fathers who wrote our Constitution and delivered our independence as a nation—the greatest assemblage of men at any time at any place in the history of the world—would be aghast at the gigantic size of our government closing in on half of all our production. They would be equally aghast at the rules and regulations and edicts handed down by a government that continues to arrogate power to itself.

We as citizens have allowed the political class to seize this power. We have allowed the left to control our schools and indoctrinate our kids with anti-American dogma. We have allowed the leftists to infiltrate almost all our cultural and economic institutions—Hollywood, schools, the churches, the universities, the arts, high tech platforms, and, of course, the media. As discussed earlier, when this capture of cultural institutions happened in Cuba, Argentina, Russia, and China, the first casualty was freedom and the second was free enterprise.

It is the duty and moral obligation of every American citizen to put at risk his or her life, liberty, and sacred honor to make sure this slide toward socialism and authoritarianism doesn't happen here. We cannot allow this surrender of freedom and liberty here, because as President Reagan reminded us, "We are the last, best hope for freedom and prosperity" on this planet. A government big enough to give you everything you want, is a government big enough to take away everything you have.

Acknowledgments

This book was written with the invaluable contributions from a whole crew of talented people dedicated to the cause of liberty. First, I want to thank Adam Brandon, president of FreedomWorks for sponsoring this project and helping fund it.

The FreedomWorks team of Jack Scheader, Paul Sapperstein, Luke Hogg, Sarah Anderson, Cesar Ybarra, Spencer Chretien, Melanie Aycock, Maddy O'Connor, and Matthew Maraist produced all of the graphics and prepared and validated all of the budget research for the book.

My friend Tom Giovanetti of Institute for Policy Innovation (IPI) in Texas allowed us the copyrights for many of the historical charts and data. This book was in part inspired by a report I prepared for IPI some two decades ago, entitled "Government: America's Number 1 Growth Industry.

Much of the key research on the debt and spending projections for the book were prepared by Zachary Cady, a research associate at the Committee to Unleash Prosperity. Erwin Antoni provided valuable economic charts for the book.

Special thanks to my friend and business partner Alexander Hoyt and my fabulous publisher Anthony Ziccardi of Post Hill Press for believing in this project and bringing this book into print under such tight deadlines for a timely release.

My wife, Anne, was my inspiration.

Made in the USA
Middletown, DE
30 October 2022

13770703R00104